"A local church can only be as healthy as its leaders. And its leaders can only be healthy when they get real. That's why I'm thrilled to recommend *Church on the Couch* to you. With an unbridled commitment to authenticity, Elaine provides practical and biblical guidance for church leaders dedicated to healing, growing, connecting, and maturing. Consider this book an essential toolbox for bringing you and the people in your care closer to each other and to God."

Les Parrott, PhD
Founder of RealRelationships.com
Author of *Trading Places*

"Getting real is a genuine option. The church is the first place it should happen. Elaine Martens Hamilton will take you there!"

John Ortberg
Pastor and Author
Menlo Park Presbyterian Church

"Elaine Hamilton has done us a great service, providing practical insights so that we can do authentic, serious discipleship in our churches. I highly recommend *Church on the Couch* to you!"

Pete Scazzero
Author of *The Emotionally Healthy Church*
Senior Pastor of New Life Fellowship Church

Church on the Couch

Does the Church Need Therapy?

Elaine Martens Hamilton

ZONDERVAN.com/
AUTHORTRACKER
follow your favorite authors

Church on the Couch
Copyright © 2009 by Elaine Martens Hamilton

Requests for information should be addressed to:
Zondervan, *Grand Rapids, Michigan 49530*

Library of Congress Cataloging-in-Publication Data

Hamilton, Elaine Martens, 1959-
    Church on the couch : does the church need therapy? /
Elaine Martens Hamilton.
        p. cm.
    Includes bibliographical references and index [if applicable].
    ISBN 978-0-310-28391-1 (softcover)
    1. Church. 2. Interpersonal relations--Religious aspects--Christianity. I. Title.
    BV600.3.H36 2008
    253.5'2--dc22
                                                                     2008025038

The names and identifying details of the individuals discussed in this book have been changed to protect their privacy.

Scripture quotations, unless otherwise indicated, are taken from the *Holy Bible, Today's New International Version™. TNIV®.* Copyright © 2001, 2005 by International Bible Society. Used by permission of Zondervan. All rights reserved.

Scripture quotations marked MSG are taken from *The Message.* Copyright © by Eugene H. Peterson 1993, 1994, 1995, 1996, 2000, 2001, 2002. Used by permission of NavPress Publishing Group.

Internet addresses (websites, blogs, etc.) and telephone numbers printed in this book are offered as a resource to you. These are not intended in any way to be or imply an endorsement on the part of Zondervan, nor do we vouch for the content of these sites and numbers for the life of this book.

All rights reserved. No part of this publication may be reproduced, stored in a retrieval system, or transmitted in any form or by any means — electronic, mechanical, photocopy, recording, or any other — except for brief quotations in printed reviews, without the prior permission of the publisher.

Interior design by Ben Fetterley

Printed in the United States of America

09 10 11 12 13 14 15 • 20 19 18 17 16 15 14 13 12 11 10 9 8 7 6 5 4 3 2 1

*To my sweet family: Ken, Katie, and Josh.
Without you, I'd still be faking it. I love you.*

Contents

	Acknowledgments	9
Introduction	My Journey to the Couch	11
Chapter 1	I'm Okay, You're Okay *Learning how to fake it*	17
Chapter 2	Analyze This *What happens when all of us fakers get together*	25
Chapter 3	Tell Me about It *Finding a way to tell our stories*	41
Chapter 4	How Does That Make You Feel? *Facing our anxiety about being real*	59
Chapter 5	Group Therapy for the Masses *Reimagining Sunday mornings*	77
Chapter 6	Defense Mechanisms Galore *Leading from an authentic place*	93
Chapter 7	Head Shrinking *Dealing with difficult people and difficult conversations*	103
Chapter 8	We've Got Issues *Handling affairs and sexual addictions*	117

Chapter 9	Analyze That	
	What authenticity looks like on the journey	131
Chapter 10	I'm Okay, No Really, I'm Okay	
	Letting yourself be human	147
Chapter 11	When Denial Is a Good Thing	
	Refusing to give up	161
	Notes	169

Acknowledgments

Thanks to:

Ernie and Pauline Owen—For telling me I still had something to say

Katya Covrett—For helping me figure out what it was I wanted to say

Leeana Tankersley—For reading every chapter more than once, providing invaluable feedback and talking me down off the ledge when necessary. This would have been so much harder without you.

To my friends and clients who bravely shared their stories. You are my heroes.

My Journey to the Couch

I come from a long line of church leaders. My mom tells me that her great grandfather was a Mennonite pastor in Russia in the 1800s. My grandparents on both sides later fled Russia to escape religious persecution and settled in Canada, along with other Mennonites. My dad and his brothers were famous for their music ministry, often singing four-part harmony over the telephone lines for their whole community. And I don't mean to brag, but I can sing the alto part of just about any hymn you can name.

When my brothers and I were young, my parents helped plant a church in rural Ontario and among the six of us, we have served in every capacity you can think of. As a family, our connection to the church and our faith has shaped so much about us.

After college, I became a missionary. I worked on high school campuses with Youth for Christ throughout my twenties. My church supported me. They sent me money and prayed for me and were always interested in what God was doing in the lives of the kids I worked with. It was a huge growing time for me and I learned a lot about relational ministry.

As I got closer to thirty, I ran out of energy for sleepovers and thought it might be time to shift to working with adults. So I decided to go to seminary to study theology in hopes of going into full-time ministry in the church. While studying there, I worked as a volunteer in women's ministries.

In the middle of all that, I met and married Ken, a handsome, fascinating guy from California, who was also in youth ministry. We hardly knew each other, having never even lived in the same country but when he asked me if I wanted to marry him and move to California, it seemed like a no-brainer. Cute guy, sandy beaches or more endless Canadian winters? Hmmm.

As one might imagine, Ken and I had a rocky start. We were both stubborn and independent and had no idea how to communicate well. Then the babies came, and the added stress plus lack of sleep made it impossible to continue to ignore the problems between us.

By this time I was in my midthirties, and the stable, focused ministry leader I had always been began to disintegrate. The advice I'd been handing out to others for years turned out to be too trite and simplistic to solve my own problems. After years of leading, I suddenly realized I had no idea where I was going anymore. And I was tired, incredibly tired. Too tired to pretend I was doing okay. I had no idea how to fix what was wrong with me. No one in my life really knew me or my struggles and, worst of all, God seemed more like a system of ideas I had studied to death than a reality I was experiencing. Another Bible study or seminary class wasn't going to fix this mess. The only thing that seemed obvious was that I needed help. I needed to get really honest, to say it all out loud to somebody and see what might come of that.

I went to see a therapist which, for me, was a big deal. I wasn't supposed to need that. That was for people who were really messed up, people who didn't know what I knew about God or the Bible. But I was sold the moment I met Sherry. She looked at me with such tenderness and listened to me so intently, I felt instantly safe. I stopped worrying about how I might look to her and focused on the work ahead of me. Sometimes she asked me to talk about painful memories; sometimes she pushed me to explore things I wanted to ignore. It was hard work but it was very, very good. She taught me that telling the truth about myself opens the door to growth. And that admitting I was struggling was far more freeing than it was humiliating.

At the time, I was leading small groups at church but longing for a place to be more honest there too. I wanted to create a new kind of group — one without particular material to study, focused rather on authentic sharing and supportive encouragement. So I approached some women and told them my plan. We began to meet and talk openly about our lives and histories. At first it was awkward. None of us was used to being this honest but I started with what was true for me. I admitted that my marriage was in crisis and that although I believed all the right things, I couldn't feel God anywhere in my life. The others followed. They shared their own painful truths—devastating childhood abuse or neglect, shameful choices, abortions, affairs. We found we had a lot in common: all trying to follow God and love our families, yet spiritually and emotionally stuck.

I'd go to therapy, then come to group and share what I was learning there about how the pain in my history was connected to the barriers in my present relationships, not only with people but with God too. We explored how this was true for each of us. The more exploring we did, the more we grew. We found that being known and accepted freed us from shame and helped us to be more loving. We started changing the way we related to our husbands, our children, our friends, and families of origin. And it opened us up in new ways to God.

Our church let us do our thing for a while but as more women were drawn to the group, church leadership told us we needed to get back to the business of running groups in more traditional ways—with clear structure and Bible study questions to answer. We tried to explain that we were actually growing, that God was changing us through what we were doing. We told them we understood for the first time what forgiveness and acceptance felt like and that we wanted to help others experience this too. They told us we were causing divisiveness by doing something different and that disunity was a tool of the devil.

Their reaction stunned me. I've always been a team player and wasn't prepared to hear that someone thought I was playing for the wrong team. I cried for a long time. Then I had to talk it through with my group. Is God really at work here? *Absolutely.* Has he called us to move forward? *Definitely.* Can we live with a few church leaders who disagree with us? *Yes.* After that, we gave up asking for the blessing of the church. And while we still participated in church, we also did our own thing—started more groups, met in our homes, wrote our own material, talked about what worked to facilitate life change, learned by trial and error. And I went back to school to study marriage and family therapy.

I'm as surprised as anyone that I am a therapist today. I didn't see it coming until it was obvious to everyone in my life but me. I never wanted to be one. But eventually I had to accept that the church was not going to come looking for me and I needed to figure out where I was going to go from here. My husband and friends had been telling me for a while that becoming a therapist was the best way to do more of what God was calling me to do. And when I finally stopped fighting it, I saw that they were right. So for the last ten years, I have been doing what I consider ministry, as a Christian therapist in private practice. Sometimes I feel like a woman without a country, shepherding people from this inbetween place, neither fully at home in the church or in my professional circles. But I've seen and experienced the transformation that comes from blending these two and, for now, this is my calling.

I don't know what to say when people ask me *if* or *how* I integrate my faith into my work as a therapist. For me it's like asking if I integrate being female into my marriage. Being a woman is what I am, how I think; being a Christian is what I am and how I think. I understand that therapy can be done from a secular perspective but for me it is a very spiritual process and provides a model for creating authentic, emotionally healthy communities. Each day my role as a therapist allows me to live out biblical concepts such as bearing the burdens of others (Gal. 6:2), weeping with those who weep (Rom. 12:15), hearing confessions of those stuck in sin (James 5:16), and bringing to light what is hidden in secret places (1 John 1:5–9). The purpose of therapy, at least for me, is to help clients learn the practice of examining their souls (Ps. 139:23–24), to look honestly and thoroughly at their relationships, their patterns of thinking and behaving (Gal. 6:4). Once this is accomplished, the work becomes about transformation — intentionally becoming someone better, stronger, more loving, more Christlike (Rom. 12:2, 10). From my perspective, this soul care is applied theology; it is applying biblical concepts to real-life situations and practicing them until they become integrated into who we are. This is the message of *Church on the Couch*. What I'm suggesting is not that everyone needs to go to therapy but that the church could benefit from incorporating therapeutic approaches that facilitate emotional health and spiritual growth.

I tell you all this because I want you to know where I come from. Sometimes, people who meet me now, as a therapist, without knowing my story, wonder about me and my faith. I don't want you to have to wonder about me. I'm a believer. I love Jesus and the Bible and I acknowledge my sinfulness and my constant, desperate need for him and his transforming power in my life. I have always been an active participant in the church. I go to church. I give to my church. I believe in the church. The fact that I have some concerns and am encouraging some changes doesn't negate any of that. I am not a critical outsider pointing at something I haven't invested in. The church is us and whatever we make of it. And I recognize that on any given day I am as likely to be part of the problem as part of the solution.

I imagine that if you've picked up this book, you are already thinking about some of the issues I will raise and that perhaps we share similar concerns. I hope you will feel validated and encouraged by what you read here. And I hope the tools and suggestions I have included will play a small part in empowering you to accomplish whatever God is calling you to in your ministry.

Chapter 1

I'm Okay, You're Okay

Learning how to fake it

> God wants us to grow up, to know the whole truth and tell it in love—like Christ in everything. We take our lead from Christ, who is the source of everything we do. He keeps us in step with each other. His very breath and blood flow through us, nourishing us so that we will grow up healthy in God, robust in love.
>
> Ephesians 4:15-16 (MSG)

STUCK IN A DARK, SCARY PLACE

One Sunday morning when I was eight years old, I got locked in a bathroom in our church basement during the service. This small country church, surrounded by pastures and cows, was over a hundred years old. The bathroom was virtually an outhouse in a dark corner underneath the sanctuary. Somehow the door jammed and I got stuck inside. I still remember the feeling of panic. It was dark and scary and really smelly and I desperately wanted out. When it became obvious I couldn't get out on my own, my panic grew. I realized I would have to bang on the door to get someone's attention. Doing that would disturb the service upstairs. That was even scarier than staying stuck. What seemed like hours passed as I weighed my fear of being trapped against my fear of causing a scene.

What do you do when you're stuck in a dark, scary place and you know you need help, but you're afraid that asking for it will only get you in trouble? Or maybe you're worried it will cause people to think less of you, or see you as weak, needy, or difficult?

I don't recall how I got out of the bathroom that day, but it must not have gone well because I remember deciding to never again be a bother—especially to the folks at church. Instead I would focus on the needs of others, ignoring my own. And I got pretty good at it. I was, in many ways, the model teenager—singing in the choir, teaching Sunday school, serving as a leader in my youth group, always encouraging others to take their faith seriously and do the right thing. Always well-behaved.

The older I got, the less aware I was of my own internal world, never expressing any doubts about my faith, never acknowledging how lonely, confused, or inadequate I felt, never revealing my struggles or self-destructive behaviors. I was doing what I thought I was supposed to do; dealing with problems on my own, trying really hard to keep it all together.

A lot of folks live like this. We keep saying to ourselves, "Don't tell people who you really are because the 'fake you' is easier to deal with." We shut down or shut out parts of ourselves that don't fit the picture of who we think we're supposed to be.

It's inevitable that this will happen to some degree. Everyone in our lives, from the time we are young, communicates subtly or not so subtly what they want from us. Experiences with parents, teachers, friends, neighbors, coaches, and church leaders all taught us what parts of us people liked and what parts they'd rather not see. Sometimes those experiences were very painful. So we learned to filter what and how much to share in order to protect ourselves from disapproval or rejection.

In his book *Abba's Child*, Brennan Manning describes this process as he experienced it. Talking about developing a false self, he writes, "When I was eight, the impostor or false self was born as a defense against pain. This impostor within whispered, 'Brennan, don't ever be your real self anymore because nobody likes you as you are. Invent a new self that everybody will admire and nobody will know.'"[1]

DEVELOPING A FALSE SELF

Children aren't born with an impostor self. They have to learn to create one. Think about the young children you know and how they function. They don't screen their feelings or reactions. They just respond. They emote and express indiscriminately, without even thinking about it. When they are happy, they're giddy, silly, grinning from ear to ear. When they are sad, they're devastated. They sob and beg and scream. But over time, the adults in their lives teach them to respond more appropriately. Children learn that people don't want them around if they are having big feelings. So they learn to tone them down, to pull themselves together, to get over it or put a lid on it. Sound familiar?

Of course, this process of shutting down emotionally doesn't end in childhood. Most of us are still experiencing life intensely in high school. Remember how passionate you felt about things then? Causes you wanted to fight for, wrongs you wanted to right, friends you went out on a limb for, the first love you were willing to give up everything for? But over time, we learned to temper our range of emotional experience, to live less passionately, to minimize the intensity, to squash it down into this small margin of acceptable expression. By the time we're in our twenties and thirties most of us have joined the ranks of grown-ups who are pretending they are fine when they are really upset, pretending that it doesn't really hurt when they are rejected or ignored, and pretending their hopes and dreams no longer matter. We've learned to deny our internal experiences in order to fit in. We've become so socially acceptable, we are emotionally dead!

I'm not suggesting that emotional restraint is all bad. Learning to control your emotions and behave appropriately is important. Certainly it is not useful or healthy to throw yourself on the floor at Starbucks when your latte isn't hot enough, or scream at your family when you've had a hard day. But it seems that what most of us learned was less about dealing with our feelings in a healthy way and more about hiding them or ignoring them till they go away.

Now we are stuck in patterns of relating we have developed to keep us safe. And while they do keep us safe (no one can reject the real us if they never see it), these patterns are killing our souls. We live mired in self-protectiveness, unable to grow, create, or experience real intimacy with God or those around us. We've begun to believe our own game and embraced our pretend self as if that's all there is to us.

THE FALSE SELF COMES TO CHURCH

Tragically, when we come together in our faith communities, we bring these coping strategies with us. We gather because we long to be known, to grow and connect with one another, but many of us are so numb and disconnected that we end up circling around each other, never quite managing to create the authentic, life-giving relationships we came for.

This book is an attempt to address our need as believers for more authenticity and emotional health, to encourage the church to lead in this area. I worry about the amount of silent pain that sits among us as we gather in our churches. I know it's there because clients tell me about it all week long in therapy sessions. Couples tell me that their marriages are falling apart; kids tell me no one really sees them, that they are using drugs, alcohol, and sex because they are in pain and are hoping someone will notice. Others tell me they are wracked by addictions to pornography, alcohol, or food. Still others are tormented by things that happened in the past, things done to them or choices they made. All this bubbles under the surface any time we get together, but in most churches there is little conversation about it. We have gotten used to being stuck and afraid together and have little or no expectation that we will experience authentic, transforming conversations with others in our faith community.

Many churchgoers are discouraged and disillusioned and some of them are leaving. They know God is the answer but they can't find what they are looking for. They are not experiencing much freedom or peace in their lives and they don't know what else to do to get it. They are exhausted from pretending and long for someone to show them the way out, to give them permission to tell the truth about their lives.

I believe that the church can be a place of amazing healing and restoration but I relate a little bit to Shawn Coyle in *To Hell with Church*:

> I quit Church for good because it is the endless rerun of a dull plot. Like Gilligan's Island, there is no character development and no learning.... In each tedious episode, like each tedious Sunday in Church, our hapless castaways almost get "saved"—but no, not quite, and so we must tune in again next week at the same bad channel, same bad time.
>
> Skipper is the pastor, Gilligan is the youth pastor, and Ginger is the one hot woman in every Church at whom all the guys steal peeps while scanning the congregation to see who showed up. Mary Ann runs the nursery, and Professor is the vaguely annoyed pseudo-intellectual who can tell you the difference between exegesis and isogesis. The Howells pay for everything. What a hoot! You just can't wait till next week to see the same thing again.
>
> Like the castaways' home, Church is a desert island on which we are trapped into playing one of just a handful of approved two-dimensional characters.[2]

Maybe you too are concerned about the lack of realness and growth within our faith communities, perhaps within yourself as well. You are not alone. I hear it from people every day. They want the church to be the one place where they don't have to fake it, but it's just not their reality. The thing I love about doing therapy is that people rarely fake it there. They sit down and tell the truth. Somehow the rules they feel elsewhere are suspended when they walk through that door. Some unsaid, invisible go-ahead allows them to put it all out there, and to expect that I will understand, accept, and protect whatever I hear. Of course, that is a therapist's job, but I am often amazed at how readily people, believing they are safe, drop their guard and share things they have never said out loud before.

I really believe this level of sharing could happen in the church if we shifted our paradigm a bit and used some different approaches and tools. My hope is to encourage you to provide opportunities for this kind of sharing. To intentionally create space for the practical living out of biblical concepts such as confession, bearing each others' burdens, and living in openness. Your community will need you to lead by example. As you risk by being a little more honest, a little more open, a little less worried about how you look, others will follow. Over time we can create a church culture that invites authentic sharing and embraces others in the middle of their struggles.

I invite you to work through the exercises and questions in each chapter. Ask some trusted friends or other leaders to join you so that you can experience firsthand the deeper sense of community that comes from sharing who you are. You can begin to create a new culture in your context, even if it begins with just a few of you.

I wish I could tell you this process will be easy or clear-cut; it won't. It will be messy and complicated, but it will be amazing too! You will feel alive and engaged, even if sometimes downright terrified. It will require more of you than you think you have to give. But it will be a great adventure! And maybe a bit more like you thought it would be to follow Jesus!

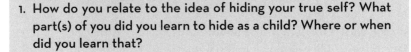

1. How do you relate to the idea of hiding your true self? What part(s) of you did you learn to hide as a child? Where or when did you learn that?

2. What parts of you do you tend to hide from others today? Why?

3. What's your reaction to the idea of living more authentically?

4. What hesitations do you have about doing that?

Chapter 2
Analyze This
What happens when all of us fakers get together

Save me, O God, for the waters have come up to my neck. I sink in the miry depths, where there is no foothold. I have come into the deep waters; the floods engulf me. I am worn out calling for help, my throat is parched. My eyes fail, looking for my God.

Psalm 69:1–3

LOSING MY WAY

As a kid, I had a thing for horses. In fact, I staged several protests during elementary school to communicate how desperately I needed one. I ran away from home twice to make my point. Both times were complete failures. When I eventually returned home, nobody had even noticed I'd been gone.

Then miraculously, when I was fifteen, we moved out to the country and my dad took me and my brothers to a nearby farm where we bought a horse. That first summer with her was a dream come true. My life became the stuff of sappy movies. We'd head off down dirt roads, through wild flowers, to the old bridge over the creek, where we'd sit for hours. Me singing John Denver tunes, wearing my twirly peasant skirt. Something about being with her connected me to God. In those hours, the concepts of God I'd been taught since childhood became a tangible reality. I told her and God all my secrets. Boy crushes, girl troubles, fights with my mom, things that scared me. And after we talked, it all faded away. I felt safe and peaceful.

I thought then that life with God would always feel this way. Long moments, day after day where right in the middle of whatever was going on, I'd be able to run away with him and feel safe.

But that's not how it happened. Eventually my life overwhelmed me. Later that year I would develop an eating disorder to deal with the sexual abuse that haunted much of my childhood. Slowly that period of peace was replaced by constant turmoil. I became less and less able to find my way back to God, less able to feel his comforting presence. I watched, powerless, as my heart drifted out to sea, out of my reach. I begged God to rescue me but by then he seemed to have disappeared too. And so I let my heart go and tried to live without it.

I adapted to living shut off from myself. As a grown-up I forgot what it was like to feel fully alive. I focused on taking care of others, doing the right thing and ignoring my own pain. And I was mostly okay. Until something came along that was too big for me. Then, oddly enough, I began to notice that I had been slowly, quietly falling apart for a long time.

At thirty-three, I was pregnant with my second child. My first pregnancy had been difficult but that darned baby girl was so cute we thought we'd have another. After months and months of throwing up every day, all day long, losing weight instead of gaining (my morning sickness is legendary in our circles), I felt myself sliding into depression. I know now that it wasn't just about how sick my body was, it was also about how sick my heart was. But at the time, all I could identify was that I was really, really sad. And angry. Life felt so meaningless. The constant nausea kept me trapped at home. I was unable to do anything—go to my classes, church, enjoy friends. Even taking care of my daughter was impossible. I felt powerless. My body had betrayed me and was holding me captive. Every day I would plead with God for some relief but none came. I counted the weeks and months, hoping that as the pregnancy progressed, things would get better. But that never happened. And even though I knew eventually it would be over, I lost perspective and began to think about dying. A lot.

It dawned on me one day that maybe I was in trouble, that perhaps the amount of time I spent wishing I was dead wasn't very healthy and

I should talk to somebody about it. But when you are a leader in your church and a seminary student, you are not supposed to be slightly suicidal. The saddest thing is not that I was struggling with depression, but that I was terrified of anyone knowing. The kinds of relationships I had then didn't include that kind of sharing. We just didn't go there. I couldn't imagine saying to anyone I knew, "I think about dying all the time." It wasn't normal to talk about things so honestly, to be raw and vulnerable. Instead, we talked about surface things—ideas, thoughts, opinions—and threw parties and organized activities. We didn't know how to share our internal worlds—our struggles, our fears, our insecurities. So, while I knew I needed help, I was too afraid to ask for it. Afraid no one in my life could handle the truth about me. More afraid that I couldn't handle hearing myself say it. Saying things out loud makes them real and I wasn't ready to be real with anyone.

TIME FOR AN HONEST ASSESSMENT

There are a lot of folks like me in your church. People who seem okay on the outside but are straining under the weight of suffocating burdens—painful marriages, shameful addictions, debilitating anxiety or depression, unrelenting guilt and negative thoughts. They don't want anyone to know because they don't want to be pitied or judged or removed from their ministry positions. They are disappointed in themselves. They thought they would be further along by now, more mature spiritually and emotionally. But everyone else seems to be doing so well, so they hide.

It's time to honestly assess what's hidden in our communities and to do this we must look closely not only at what we can see on Sunday mornings or during our events and programs but at what's going on in their lives. How are those who attend our churches really doing? Are they experiencing transformation, enjoying a life-giving connection with God and the people in their lives? Over the last fifteen years I have had hundreds of conversations with believers from various faith communities in different parts of the country and their stories reflect a common condition.

HERE'S WHAT THEY TELL ME
1. Many of our people feel stuck.

While people are involved in their churches—attending Bible studies and small groups and serving—they are not experiencing much internal change. Acceptance, forgiveness, joy, and peace are simply intellectual concepts to them, not part of their everyday reality. The abundant life promised in Scripture feels like some kind of get-you-in-the-door sales pitch. These men and women long to integrate authentic Christianity into their lives but don't know how. And despite all the ideas and strategies they have tried that are supposed to create spiritual growth, they still feel disconnected from God and see themselves as spiritual failures who are a disappointment to him.

As a result, marriages are falling apart at the same rate as for people who don't attend church. Too many of our kids are angry and disconnected from their families. In growing numbers we are addicted to food, pornography, television, and money. We've got to be honest with ourselves: an intellectual understanding of faith issues does not equal spiritual maturity. An ability to discuss doctrinal issues does not equal an intimate relationship with God or a transformed life. Knowing about God, even knowing a lot about God, does not guarantee growth.

Spiritual maturity is most meaningfully demonstrated by a believer's growth in his or her ability to love. Not preach, teach, or lead, but love. Jesus was clear that our greatest mandate is to increase our capacity to love him and each other. And that is more likely to happen in communities where folks are pursuing emotional health; where honesty, interdependence, and restoration are valued; where biblical concepts such as confession, bearing one another's burdens, walking in the truth, and repentance are really being lived out; where theology is practically applied, rather then merely discussed. If this is our measuring stick, then we would be asking different questions, questions like:

- What's going on in our homes?
- Are husbands, wives, and children managing their anger well?
- Do they feel safe emotionally and physically with each other?

- Are our kids connected enough to the adults in their lives to talk about their doubts and stresses and bad choices?
- Are our single parents embraced and encouraged?
- Do our elderly feel known and valued?
- Is it normative for our people to share struggles and doubts with one another?

The question isn't how many small groups we have or what kind of programs we offer, but what is actually happening in the lives of our people.

In *The Emotionally Healthy Church*, Peter and Geri Scazzero talk about the connection between emotional health and spiritual maturity. They share how a crisis in their marriage forced them to face their own emotional condition, radically changing not only their relationship but the way they do ministry. Peter says of their journey:

> Embracing the truth about the emotional parts of myself unleashed nothing short of a revolution in my understanding of God, Scripture, the nature of Christian maturity, and the role of the church. I can no longer deny the truth that emotional and spiritual maturity are inseparable....
>
> Despite all the emphasis today on spiritual formation, church leaders rarely address what spiritual maturity looks like as it relates to emotional health, especially as it relates to how we love other people....
>
> Unless we integrate emotional maturity with a focus on loving well into our discipleship, we are in danger of missing God's point completely—love.[3]

It's difficult to take people farther than we have gone ourselves. If we are not growing in our own ability to love—if our own spouses, children, family, and friends have a hard time feeling loved by us—it is unlikely we are offering anything authentic when it comes to developing spiritual maturity in others. I don't mean by that, that our relationships must be perfect or running smoothly at all times. Mine certainly aren't. But we can't ignore them nor can we fake it.

I know it's a tall order for leaders. I feel the tension too. What do I do when I'm presenting a workshop about conflict in marriage and I broke all the rules the night before? Or when I'm an "expert" on a parenting seminar panel and I'd like to crawl under the table because today I don't have a clue about what to do with one of my kids? The good news is, everybody has days like this. Days when they don't know what the heck they're doing. So we might as well just say so. Just put it out there. "Today I was a lousy wife," "Today I want to sell my children to the gypsies." It's not earth shattering. It's just real life, and anyone who's honest experiences it.

Your church doesn't need you to be perfect, they just need you to be real and to be in the battle with them.

2. Many of us are medicating ourselves instead of dealing with our pain.

I started binge eating at age fifteen. I don't remember making a choice to use food to make myself feel better. I had no idea why I wanted to eat so much more than my body needed, I just knew it comforted me. By the time I was in college, I was eating every day until I could no longer swallow, then taking large amounts of laxatives to purge. I woke up sick every morning and went to bed sick every night. I couldn't purge fast enough and began to put on weight. I felt ugly, ashamed, and guilty all the time but powerless to stop. I begged God to change me, but no rescue came. I never told anyone what I was doing. Food became both my most trusted friend and my most relentless enemy, and it would be many years before I could free myself from it.

The worst part of being bulimic was not knowing why I was doing it. Nothing was wrong with my life. I was doing well in school, involved in my church, had a busy social life, a family who loved me, and yet ... something was terribly wrong. It wasn't until I was in my late twenties, sitting in a class, that I first heard about the connection between bulimia and sexual abuse. I finally understood that I had been trying to distract myself from the pain of that experience in my childhood. And food was my drug of choice.

My uncle tormented me when no one was looking. He spied on me, said disgusting things to me, touched me. And I never told anyone. Like most children who are abused, I believed it was my fault, that I would be blamed if I told, or that no one would believe me. That would be worse than bearing it alone, so I pretended I was okay. Then I discovered that food helped numb the pain. So I learned to swallow it all—the shame, the terror, the humiliation all disappeared if I ate enough.

It doesn't matter what you use to medicate yourself or what you are trying to escape from, the game is the same. It's all about finding something to take away the pain, to avoid the gnawing ache inside you that says something is wrong, something needs attention. But the "something" is too overwhelming to look at. In the beginning, the medicators bring relief, protecting you from what you can't face, but ultimately they control you and shut down your soul. And yet, it's easier than living with the alternative. Better to feel like a loser because you ate a bag of cookies than to deal with a painful history. Better to keep frantically busy than acknowledge the rejection you feel in your relationships. Better to waste days, weeks, months watching TV or Internet porn, or drinking a little too much, or working too hard than to try one more time to create change in your life.

On those dark days when I am using food, I am sure of one thing: I am a complete and utter failure. I hear Satan's voice: "This is all you will ever be. This weak, self-destructive mess is the real you. You are so pathetic. You have nothing to offer and you will never be free." The message is so strong and I've heard it so often, it seems as if it must be true.

It sounds bad, doesn't it? And I would be too embarrassed to put it down in black and white if it weren't for this: I know I am not alone. I know others hear the voice too. They tell me their stories, their ugly, humiliating truth. How trapped and out of control they feel, how many times they've tried to change and failed. I tell them they are not alone. That we are all in the same boat. Underneath our competence and independence and talent, a lot of us are in pain and a lot of us are self-medicating.

Maybe we could begin talking about this in church. Maybe, if we go first, it could become normal for us all to tell the truth. The truth is not so terrible, you know. Not once it's been exposed to the light. I've seen it happen. Groups of people gathered together, sharing their stories. At first they're scared to death, sure they will be rejected when they tell others who they really are. But they begin, and then the miracle happens. The others breathe a collective sigh. They nod and smile and say, "Me too. I've felt that. I've made stupid choices too!" And then they finally know they are not alone. Knowing that others relate frees them to move forward, allows them to confront their sin with strength rather than shame. That's when growth begins to happen.

3. We are hurting each other.

We are all leading from wounded places and that's okay as long as we know that about ourselves. When we know our issues, we can try to protect people from them, or at least apologize when we screw up. But when we deny we have any issues, we can be downright dangerous. Too many of us don't realize we are controlling, judgmental, dismissive, sarcastic, arrogant. And because we are in positions of authority, people are afraid to tell us. Without their feedback, we carry on, evaluating only what we can see — attendance is up, programs are running, special events are successful. But what may be missing is personal transformation — in ourselves and our people. We have failed to create a place where woundedness is addressed, struggles are verbalized, and comfort and support are experienced.

I'm working with a young man who's interning at a church while attending seminary. Matt is a unique and remarkable human being. More gifts than three or four regular folks put together. But after three years of ministry, he's had enough of the church and is ready to leave for good. He's been trying to live authentically, to be honest about his doubts and struggles — but in his context, that's a mistake. He's been labeled, avoided, and dismissed. He's been hurt badly and consistently. He's come to therapy to figure out who's crazy — him or his church.

I asked Matt to put his feelings on paper, to vent without censoring himself, to just let fly with all the disappointment, confusion, and anger (hence all the bad words!). He read it to me the next session and it was a heartbreaking lament, reminding me of one of King David's psalms. He said I could share it with you.

> I have so much self-doubt, wondering if I'll ever be good enough for anyone. I feel crazy, like I'm losing my mind, confused because my thoughts make sense to me but when they come out, no one understands me. I hate this place, these a — holes that snicker and laugh at anyone who is different, who thinks differently, who is bold enough to be honest with their questions. Why the hell would I want to be a Christian if it means mocking all others? It's not very good strategy to disrespect those you are hoping to convert.
>
> I feel there is so little left of me here. I've got nothing more to give to these soul-destroying people. I'm so terrified to do anything in the Christian world because I am scared I'll just keep being kicked and knocked down. I do not want people to be abused anymore. I can't take it. I'm tired of believing I'm crazy, that I suck, that I'm weird, abnormal. I'm tired of believing there is something wrong with me. I'm so afraid, with all my pondering, to let people know who I really am ... especially Christians. I can't do it if this arrogant mockery, this hurtful reaction is normative.
>
> I feel like the only way I can do that is to not think, not speak, in essence, become something other than the only way I currently know how to be. I'm not talking of simply being self-controlled. I can be controlled. But I cannot stay quiet about social intolerance in the name of Christ. I cannot stay quiet about racism, about sexism, about political agendas and control, about blatant dishonesty and inauthentic people. I cannot stay silent because I am driven by some force within me to cry out in the name of love for some compassion, some care, some gentle understanding. I have to scream for some grace. I can't take this bulls — t anymore.
>
> My perspective of God is so f — ked up because my witnesses, my teachers, my parents, my Christian world will never be pleased with me. I'll never live up to their standards. Why? Why are these people like this? Why do I continually seek to prove myself to them, try to live up to their standards and be humiliated again and again, punched and

broken. I know and believe that God is gracious, loving, etc. But I don't live with any freedom. How does one unlearn such permeating lies? How can I break free from the lies I am telling myself subconsciously? Will the pain ever stop?

Am I mad at God for all this? Wondering why he lets all this happen to me? Is this his fault? Does he free me from my chains or sit mocking me like all the others? Why don't I feel your love, your grace? Why do I hurt so much? I give you all I know how to give. Why am I wrestling with you so? Will the morning ever come or will I come undone in this nightmare of life you put me in? Let me wake up, please let me be free from the dark and painful reality that creeps in on me every second of every day. Will you torment me forever? Is this my fault? Something I am not doing right? Are you any different than them? Do you even care? Are you even there? Am I blinded by myself? I am so confused, so broken and distressed. I feel as if I am drowning, but you just watch safely from the shore as I scream. You do not come in. You are indifferent to my fear, to my slow death. . . .

I cannot believe this of you. I just hurt so bad and have no adequately satisfactory conclusion!

I want to cry for young people like Matt. He has so much to offer, and if he is loved and believed in, he can change the world. But he has too much integrity to stay in a sick system. He's not going to be able to look the other way and focus on the tasks of ministry. He really believes a relationship with Jesus is supposed to change a person's life and he'd rather leave than settle.

I wish Matt's experience was unusual, but it's not. Most of my clients are believers and they express similar sentiments — a confusion about whether God is like the people who represent him: Is he as demanding and disappointed, as frustrated with us as the significant people in their lives are? I feel like I'm constantly trying to clean up God's reputation, trying to separate him from their negative experiences with others.

To be fair, I know that this is inevitable, that no matter how good our intentions, we will sometimes fail each other. I'd love to believe that my own stuff isn't hurting anybody but that's just fairy-tale thinking.

We will forever be poor reflections of God—but if we could just admit it, talk about it, take responsibility for it, we would do far less damage.

We have wasted too much time being intellectual about God—studying ideas and concepts, debating over interpretations—and far too little on how to actually integrate these concepts into how we live. And it shows. We have highly trained, talented leadership and yet we are leading people in circles. Yes, folks are showing up, involved in programs, and serving but they don't know how to look each other in the eye and talk about their struggles with their kids, or their anger, or their grief, or their disappointment with God. They don't know how to tolerate painful conversations, or how to support each other in the middle of a crisis. Instead, they feel lost and stuck and find it necessary to look outside the church for help with these issues.

4. Our strategies sometimes sabotage the development of meaningful relationships.

Take a look at how churches tend to try to stimulate growth. Often it's big programs that involve a lot of people listening to an expert, with little opportunity to interact with each other. While the content of these programs may be relevant, without the chance to process and practice new concepts, integration rarely happens.

Even small groups, which offer the opportunity for practical application, are often paced to cover a specific amount of material. For some, the idea of group members talking at length about real-life issues is "getting off track." These groups are content driven, often designed to be short-term, ending after a few months. Then someone "blows the whistle" and participants are reshuffled into new groups, to get to know a new group of people. As a result, conversations remain intellectual, superficial, or others oriented, and people rarely feel safe enough to talk about real problems. Expressed prayer requests often are for people who aren't there, or aren't known to the group. We end up discussing the needs of relatives or neighbors, not our own.

I don't want to suggest that these kinds of groups don't meet any needs, because certainly they do. They provide an opportunity for people to meet and begin to relate, a chance to feel a part of the larger community and see who they might click with. But in order to grow emotionally healthy people, we must offer something that goes deeper. It's important to take an honest look at the results our programs are producing. Are people really building meaningful, "iron sharpens iron" relationships? Do they know each other's histories and current struggles? Ask your group leaders and group members what level of sharing is going on.

Jesus was all about relationships over the long haul, developing intimacy and trust over time. He handpicked his group, even held a meeting to make it official (Luke 6:12–16). He spent almost every waking hour for three years with the same group of guys. They did life together, knew each others' stories, habits, weaknesses, and strengths.

Jesus' model with his disciples would be considered cliquey and exclusive by many churches today. So many of us are living such isolated and disconnected lives that when we see that kind of connection we are bothered by it. We either want in or we want to make it go away. Often such groups are a target for suspicion or jealousy. Their existence makes others feel left out so there must be something wrong with them.

Think about it. How often have you heard or felt something negative about a group of folks who belong to one another? Or been criticized yourself for being a part of an identifiable group? We have been doing this since high school, right? Somebody else's inclusion emphasizes our own lack of belonging. We want it but we can't figure out how to get it, so we decide nobody should have it. We arrange it so that no one has to feel left out. Everyone gets a little, no one gets a lot. What no one ever talks about is the investment these folks have made in each other. Or how beautiful it is that they accept and support one another through thick and thin. We focus instead on how it impacts those of us who haven't been able to create it. I'm not saying we do this on purpose, but we end up so busy trying to be fair and inclusive that we actually sabotage any opportunity to experience what we all really need. Our own gang.

I know that Jesus' strategy was about trying to change the world but in my own small way, that's what I'm trying to do too. And I need my little gang to do it. People who have known me for years, lived life with me, been there in the suffering and in the glory and know what to do with me—know when I need encouragement and when I need a kick in the pants—know when I'm just venting, and that I'm not really going to run over my husband with a truck or sell my children to the gypsies.

You can't get this kind of intimacy moving to new groups every few months, or every year. I don't care about being known by everyone; I care about being known by a few trusted friends who are invested in each other. Some might complain I'm not inclusive enough but I'm not trying to win Miss Congeniality. (Though I did win Miss Valentine Baking Contest of 1975 at my high school and that was kind of thrilling.) I'm on a mission. I want to help create real, lasting, freeing change in the lives of a few, rather than a lot of nothing in the lives of many.

The next time someone decides it's time for small groups to be reshuffled, I hope you will ask some tough questions of yourself and of those in charge. Does this make sense? Is our strategy producing life change? Are people growing and connecting with one another in ways that are transforming, or do we need to do this differently?

All around you are folks who want more. They need opportunities to commit long-term to someone, to live life together for a while, to learn about each other over time, to experience the freedom of being known and accepted with all their secrets and shame.

YOUR TURN

1. How did you react to this chapter? What did you agree with? What did you disagree with?

(cont.)

2. Do you struggle with using something to medicate yourself? What are you trying to avoid when you do it?

3. How have you been hurt by people in the church? What do you do to avoid getting hurt now?

Chapters 3 and 4 focus on creating a specific kind of small group—process groups. I believe strongly that effective small groups are essential to building a healthy, authentic community. I've included tools to help generate significant sharing as well as suggestions for managing this kind of group and dealing with potential problems. Even just a couple of effective process groups can be a powerful change agent in your church as a whole. Once people hear that connection and growth are happening in these groups, even those who are resistant tend to become more open.

Chapter 3

Tell Me about It

Finding a way to tell our stories

> "You don't get wormy apples off a healthy tree, nor good apples off a diseased tree. The health of the apple tells the health of the tree. You must begin with your own life-giving lives. It's who you are, not what you say and do, that counts. Your true being brims over into true words and deeds."
>
> Luke 6:43-45 (MSG)

START WITH THE TRUTH

At a recent conference, author and speaker Gordon MacDonald shared that for several years he and his wife have been meeting with groups of fifteen people once a week for forty weeks. During the forty weeks, each participant shares a detailed version of their life story. Every issue of brokenness under the sun has come up at some point. MacDonald said he's been humbled by "how much blood there was in the pew.... I spent all this time in church leadership grossly underestimating the depth of pain and hurt in the lives of my people."

But how do we create authentic, emotionally healthy communities? How do we change the culture of our church? We begin by telling the truth about ourselves and providing opportunities for others to do the same. Changing the culture of a church is a huge job but your people will follow your lead. If you show them what it looks like to reveal parts of yourself, they will begin to do the same. Modeling authenticity is the most effective way to teach it.

It's the difference between a leader talking about a concept, like controlling one's anger, and what my pastor did one Sunday morning when he confessed that he'd "lost it" with one of his kids and tried to force-feed her a banana. Even if we don't remember everything he said that morning, nobody will forget the story or the level of honesty they experienced. Rather than a three-point sermon about how to be self-controlled, his story got our attention. It woke us up and connected us to him and to our own struggles. His vulnerability communicated that it's okay to admit we make mistakes — we all do. And it reminded us that our weaknesses are causing pain in the lives of those we love. Why is this level of self-revelation necessary? Because it's the truth — about us and the people we lead. In some kind of way, we are all shoving a banana in somebody's face, so maybe we should just admit it.

Still this is not easy. Last month I spoke at a marriage retreat and Ken was invited to come with me. We had had a couple of terrible weeks prior to the retreat, and neither of us was sure we wanted to spend the weekend together. We argued on the way, and by the time we got there, I just wanted him to drop me off and go home. I felt humiliated beginning our first session, all these young couples looking to me for direction, and my husband there in the crowd knowing who I am and what I am capable of (and I don't mean that in a good way). I wanted to run screaming from the room, "I can't do this!" But they had already handed me a check, so I started off by telling the truth. That marriage is hard and that sometimes it feels too hard, that Ken and I struggle, and that perhaps the biggest reason we are still together after twenty-some years is that both of us are just too stubborn to give up.

Living authentically means I can't say, "Let me tell you what to do about your life," and leave out the fact that I'm having a heck of a time in my own. It *doesn't* mean I have to share every gruesome detail with everyone, but I need to be honest enough to communicate that I'm a fellow struggler. Because whether I acknowledge it or not, I am.

Here, however, is the dilemma of leading the way to authenticity. While it can be freeing and stimulate all kinds of growth in you and your community, some folks will be unhappy. Not everyone will like you if you are this honest. Some people will be very disappointed that you are not all together. That your marriage, your kids, your thought life, your reactions are not perfect. They need to believe you've got your life together because they are pretending the same about their own. And from their perspective, it's easier to follow you if you are not really going anywhere. I find that these people will ultimately wander off, or storm off, when they sense you are serious about actual transformation. Try not to spend too much energy trying to convince them to come along; they will only be annoyed or threatened by your passion. They may even begin to refer to you (in a loving Christian way, of course) as a tool of the devil. (Sorry, I'm still not over it. See introduction.)

Fortunately, plenty of folks recognize their need for more authentic relationships, will find your vision and self-disclosure relieving and inspiring, and will follow you to the ends of the earth! So let's just go for it. Let's live like we believe that loving Jesus should change our lives. Besides, faking it only lasts so long and eventually, no matter how hard you try to cover up your stuff, your flaws will be revealed at some point. I say, better to put your own head on the chopping block and hope for mercy than to have someone do it for you.

TELLING OUR STORIES

Our stories connect us to one another and to ourselves. Telling you what I've experienced and how I feel about it invites you to experience the real me and helps me figure myself out as well. Most people express a fear that their struggles are unique, that others don't feel the same kinds of feelings or make the same mistakes. And yet when people begin to share their stories, inevitably they see how similar we all are. The details of our histories might differ, but the ways in which we have reacted and the patterns we have developed because of them are much the same. Being controlling or distant or people-pleasing are all coping strategies, all about the same thing—protecting our hearts from further hurt. Talking about our histories helps us work together to see how our past and our present are connected, which in turn opens the door to healing and growth.

For example, when someone opens up about their childhood abuse it's easier to understand their present difficulty with trusting others. It makes sense then that they would have trouble trusting when they've been so betrayed in the past. Making these connections helps us figure out how to relate to one another. If I know that you become controlling or distant when you feel threatened, I understand your behavior. I don't have to take it personally. Instead, I can move *toward* you, ask what is triggering your behavior, and how I can help you feel safe. Then you have the opportunity to choose how to respond rather than staying stuck in a self-protective mode. The result—both of us are growing.

In the early days of my first group, I admitted that while I desperately wanted deeper relationships, I rarely got close to other women. I had always blamed that on not finding the right person or not having enough time but I was beginning to realize I wasn't really open to a significant friendship. When I considered why I was behaving as I did, I discovered I was afraid—afraid that I would never really matter to someone else. Being a leader instead of one of the group was my way of securing a place of importance. As I talked about this, I remembered feeling the same way as a young girl. I told my group the following story from my childhood.

There were two girls in my neighborhood with whom I spent a lot of time over the years. Anna and Brenda were best friends. They lived beside each other, their moms made them matching outfits and arranged for them to be in the same classroom every year. The three of us often played together and rode bikes to school together—Anna first, Brenda second, me last. They were never mean to me, never rubbed it in my face, they just belonged to each other in a way that I did not. They had a special relationship that I was not a part of. And while they are not responsible for my feelings, I learned then that I was irrelevant. While I could be accepted at some level, I was not in the inner circle. I was an unnecessary part of the picture. And I had carried that baggage with me into my adulthood—the belief that while other women might belong to each other, I was just extra.

I felt humiliated telling the story that day. It felt so silly, so ridiculous to still be feeling sad about something that happened so long ago and yet it was still with me, impacting the ways I engaged, or better, failed to engage, in friendships. But once it was out there, I also felt relieved that I had said it out loud and now the other group members knew the truth about me. They said they understood, that my reaction made sense, and that they hoped I would come to understand how important I was to them. That helped a lot but it was not all they did.

My girlfriends in the group came up with a plan to help me. They began to put me in the middle. Physically in the middle. When we would go to the movies, or dinner, when we would walk down the street together, they would put me in the middle. At first I squirmed and tried to get out of formation. I told them they didn't need to baby me because of my ridiculous insecurity. But they ignored my protests (as they often do when they know they are right and I am wrong). And over time, something changed. That action on their part healed something inside me. Something I never expected to feel, ever, is now very solid inside me. I know, I mean really know, that I belong to them, and that I mean as much to them as they do to me. Not only does this feel great, it also empowers me. It allows me to love them freely, without hesitation. I'm not afraid that I will become invisible or that something I do will end the relationship. Certainly I might disappoint or hurt them from time to time but because we are committed to each other, I know we'll talk it out. I don't have to brace myself for some inevitable rejection. I also don't worry much about being rejected by other folks because I've got them. I need less from others because I have a safe place to come home to. That allows me to love and care for others without worrying if they will love me back. Maybe they will, maybe they won't — but either way, I've got my gang so I'm okay.

A NEW KIND OF GROUP

Creating this kind of authenticity and vulnerability requires intentionality, but it can happen in both structured and unstructured ways. For instance, you could begin by pulling together a couple of other friends and simply meet regularly to share what's going on in your lives. However, when we are just learning to relate vulnerably, it can be useful to create structured environments where the purpose is clearly stated.

If running this kind of group or experience is new to you, consider the differences between traditional learning groups and process learning experiences (see Figure 1, page 47). In short, traditional learning could describe what usually happens in group Bible studies or in teaching settings. Process learning environments have a different goal: to deal with the material (the stories, experiences, concerns) that each person brings to the group rather than material that the leader presents to the group. The leader functions as a facilitator and participant in the group rather than an expert. Ownership and responsibility for the success of the group belongs to the group members themselves.

Celebrate Recovery and Twelve Steps are both examples of process groups that many churches commonly offer. In each participants are expected to talk openly about their struggles. Group members are not shocked to hear about someone's difficult childhood or painful marriage or poor choices. Leaders acknowledge their own brokenness and lead as fellow strugglers. While these groups are often focused on a particular issue, such as alcoholism or sexual addiction, the same principles can be applied to general process groups, where members are bonded together by their shared commitment to deal with a variety of life issues.

Process learning can happen in small and large groups. Starting a process group will require well-defined goals and objectives. Because people are generally more accustomed to traditional learning settings, it's important to be straightforward and state at the outset what kind of group this will be. I suggest screening group members, meeting individually with potential members to get a sense of what they are looking for and clarifying that their goals coincide with those of the group.

If you sense that someone is not ready for this type of experience or that their lack of social skills may damage the group, refer them to some other program your church has to offer, possibly a mentoring or a classroom situation. While most people can learn to do well in a process group, some will not and will end up holding the group captive because they are volatile, mean-spirited, or insensitive to others.

I like to use a covenant at the beginning of each new group to introduce and discuss our shared purpose. Putting the terms in writing adds

FIGURE 1: Traditional Learning vs. Process Learning

Traditional Learning

Roles are defined; leaders teach, members listen and learn.

The leader is "the authority." He must be an "expert" and command the respect of members. He provides all the answers. Learning is based on his authority, knowledge, and command of content.

Members work with external and abstract data (content) provided by the leader. The leader defines what needs to be learned.

Members seek to know themselves by measuring themselves against an ideal type. They are externally oriented to performing for the expectations of others.

Major learning problems involve the accumulation and storage of external information and the acquisition of "right answers." Motivation is difficult, and memory difficulties destroy effectiveness.

Process Learning

Roles are determined by involvement and interaction. Leaders can be learners; members can be teachers.

The leader helps to formulate problems and assists in the development of problem-solving skills. He helps others "learn how to learn." Learning is based on each member's commitment/ involvement in the learning process. Each member develops personal problem-solving skills.

Members work with external *and* internal data. Members determine what they need to learn. Members consult the leader for assistance.

Members seek to know themselves by the choices they make, the relationships they enter, and the knowledge they seek. They are internally oriented and establish their own performance standards.

Major learning problems involve communication (increasing understanding), involvement (participation), and transparency (vulnerability). The emphasis on developing problem-solving skills maintains motivation to learn and acquire relevant knowledge.

Adapted from *Introduction to Psychology and Counseling: Christian Perspectives and Applications*, Paul D. Meier (Grand Rapids, Mich.: Baker Publishing Group, 1982). Used by permission.

weight to the experience, helping members understand we are taking the group seriously and expect something meaningful to come of it. The sample group covenant (see Figure 2, page 49) focuses on not only the purpose of the group but also the importance of attending each week, participating openly, and maintaining confidentiality to create safety. I give a copy to each person and have them sign and keep it to serve as a reminder of the commitment they are making to themselves and each other. We want participants to understand that showing up, contributing to the conversation, and keeping confidences are required of everyone and necessary for the success of the group.

I urge you to talk about confidentiality for at least the first several weeks and then give occasional reminders. Maintaining confidences is something most of us are not good at, so it is important everyone understands that the information they learn about each other is private and never to be passed on — not even to a spouse and not even for purposes of prayer. While they are free to talk about their own stuff and what they are learning about themselves outside the group, other people's stuff is strictly off-limits. What happens here, stays here. (Kind of like Vegas, only in a good way.) Nothing kills a group faster than a breach of privacy.

TOOLS FOR GETTING YOUR GROUP STARTED

Begin with each member telling their story — what their family was like, significant life experiences and relationships, and so on. Suggest an amount of time you'd like each person to take for their story, perhaps twenty minutes or so. Depending on the number of people in the group (I like six to eight), this could take several weeks.

Generally, people are not accustomed to talking about themselves for this long in a group setting so they will need help with what to share. Some options for sharing are presented over the remainder of this chapter. You could use any one of these exercises or a combination thereof. Genograms, for example, give people an opportunity to look very thoroughly at their family of origin, exploring characteristics, patterns, and themes. However, because of the intensity of the exercise, genograms may be better used once a greater atmosphere of safety exists

FIGURE 2: Sample Group Covenant

Purpose of Our Group:

- To grow in our relationships with God and others by sharing, exploring, supporting, and caring for one another.
- To address any areas of our lives that are hindering our spiritual growth and relationships with others.

Attending:
We agree to make this group a priority and will commit ourselves to attending each meeting with the exception of significant extenuating circumstances. We will let others know if we are unable to attend.

Participating:
We agree to participate by sharing openly and allowing ourselves to be vulnerable. We will provide a safe place for other group members by refraining from advice-giving (unless asked) or judging.

Maintaining Confidentiality:
We agree to respect each other's privacy and commit to keeping what is said in the group in strict confidence. While we are free to talk about what we are learning or discovering about ourselves with others outside the group, we will not share any information regarding other members. We understand this is imperative to the success of our group experience.

I accept the conditions of this covenant and commit myself to this group. I understand that I am committed to this group from (dates) _____ to _____. If, during the course of this time, I become unable or unwilling to remain in the group, I will personally communicate with the group my concerns or reasons for leaving.

Name _____ Date _____

within the group. On the other hand, if the group is already comfortable together, genograms are an ideal way to deepen the level of intimacy, so you may want to plunge right in.

Getting-to-Know-You Questions

One of the simplest approaches to sharing personal stories is to give group members a list of questions to address as they talk about themselves. If they are hesitant about sharing this much information right off the bat, present one or two of the questions each week and have the whole group respond. Here are some sample questions:

- What was your family of origin like?
- How did people get along in your family when you were young? What are those relationships like now?
- What were you like as a kid, a high schooler?
- What significant experiences/relationships did you have in high school/college?
- What has your spiritual journey been like?
- What are you struggling with today?
- What are your goals right now? What are you hoping to get out of the group?

Remind your group that the goal is not to solve anyone's problems or to make people feel better about what has happened to them. We are just going to listen and validate. We may ask questions if we are confused but we may not express opinions or jump in with our own stories during someone else's turn.

Timelines

On a large piece of paper draw a long line marked off in five-year intervals. Then take some time to think about any significant relationships or events that occurred during each five-year span. Take up to a week to work on your timeline. Don't worry about time spans where you have few memories. This is not unusual, particularly if there is abuse in your history. You may want to look at photos of yourself throughout the years to help jog your memory. When you're finished, share your timeline with your group. If you used photos, bring them along. Talk about not only the events that occurred but any feelings you remember having when they occurred. For example, if your parents divorced, did you feel scared, responsible, confused, relieved? (See Figure 3, page 52, for a sample timeline.)

Timelines provide a way for people to present their histories in a visual, chronological way and work very well for people who might need more structure. They also are helpful for people who have few memories of their childhood. Coming up with just one memory for each five-year period usually helps bring others to the surface.

Genograms

Genograms are a sort of family tree. You will map out two or three generations of your family: (1) you and your siblings, (2) your parents and their siblings, and (3) your grandparents and their siblings. If you don't know all of these people, consider getting information from your parents or other relatives. If that is not doable, just fill in the details as best you can. Then add two to three characteristics describing each of those people, especially the ones who had the biggest impact on your life. Use symbols or words to indicate what kind of relationship you had with significant members, and what kind of relationships they had with each other (see Figure 4, page 53). Focus on the status of those relationships during your childhood and adolescence.

Figure 5 (page 54) shows the first step in completing a genogram. Start by drawing out your two or three generations. In the sample, Claire has drawn out her parents, Keith and Lola, and her sister Molly. Above that she's drawn her grandparents, Byron and Mary and Fred and Polly and their children. She's done the same with her husband and his family. Once all the players are drawn out, add in symbols and characteristics to describe each person and relationship to help you examine patterns and relating styles within your family. You could also add another generation.

FIGURE 3: "Steve's" Timeline

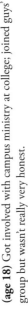

- **(age 5)** Mom and Dad fought a lot, scared me.
- **(age 7)** Second-grade teacher was very encouraging, made me feel smart.
- **(age 8)** Found Dad's porn, felt curious and bad.
- **(age 10)** Mom and Dad divorced, didn't see Dad much after that.
- **(age 13)** Was invited to youth group with a friend. Became a Christian. Lots of fun, but no one really knew me.
- Played football throughout high school. Felt like I belonged during football season.
- I was always trying to please the coach. He was tough but fair. Dad would sometimes come to games. That was a big deal.
- **(age 16)** First sexual experience — felt like I pressured the girl a little.
- **(age 18)** Got involved with campus ministry at college; joined guys' group but wasn't really very honest.
- Worked as a leader in campus ministry throughout college, led men's groups. Other men confessed porn use but no one knew what to do. Slipped and had sex a few times during college — felt shame about that.
- **(age 23)** Offered dream job at corporation. Focused on career, worked long hours.
- **(age 25)** Met wife, really excited about the relationship.
- **(age 27)** Married, thought that would end my struggle with porn.
- **(Early 30s)** Started a home group for couples, comfortable in leadership roles, have always done it.
- **(age 34)** Confessed porn use to wife. Feel shame, fear she may leave. Feel helpless, have no relationships where I can get help with this.

Years 0 5 10 15 20 25 30 35

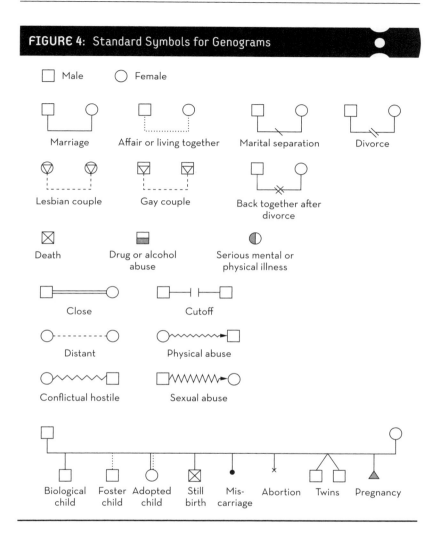

FIGURE 4: Standard Symbols for Genograms

In our next sample, Figure 6 (page 55), Claire has described her relationship with her husband, Mitch, as emotionally unavailable or distant. Her relationship with her father is also distant, but she feels close to her mother. Claire's mother (Lola) has had a conflictual or hostile relationship with Claire's father (Keith). Lola remarried and is close to her new husband. On Mitch's side of the genogram, we see a distant

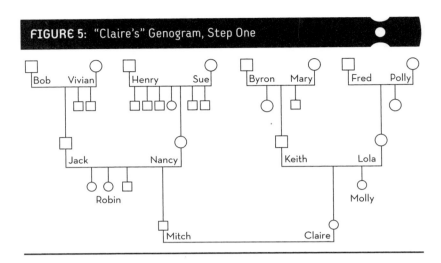

FIGURE 5: "Claire's" Genogram, Step One

relationship with his dad, who abuses drugs or alcohol and has had a series of affairs. And so on.

Collage

For some people, telling their story abstractly is far less threatening. Using pictures and words from magazines or childhood photos, create a collage that represents your life thus far: how you feel about yourself, how you see yourself, what you are struggling with. You could also draw or paint pictures or write words that describe you or your feelings. See Figure 7, page 56, for an example of a collage. Suzanna, the seventeen-year-old "artist," described it this way:

> *There's a girl in a canoe, attempting to make her way up a waterfall. This past year, this waterfall has been my life. With school, boys, parents, and everything else, everything was just overwhelming me. I felt like I was in over my head. To top it all off, there were signs coming from every direction, telling me to go different ways, none of them very clear. And girls who I thought were my friends were talking about all my problems behind my back. I felt isolated and judged. It tore*

Tell Me about It   55

FIGURE 6: "Claire's" Genogram, Completed

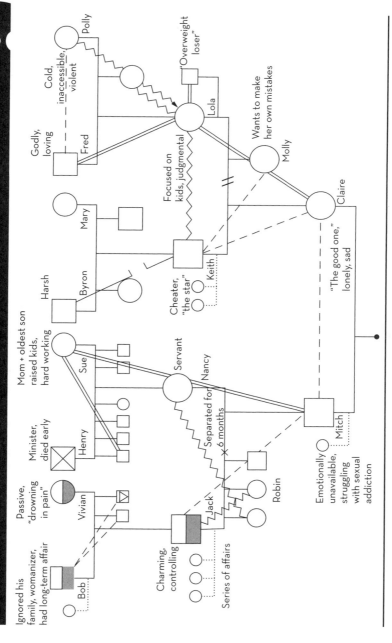

FIGURE 7: "Suzanna's" Collage

me apart. Whenever I was around them I felt like I was walking on eggshells, trying not to do or say anything that could start another round of rumors. And then when it escalated to total isolation, I felt like nothing, worthless. It felt as though I was in a sea of people, all moving around me, but no one noticing the hurt that I was enduring. I couldn't be heard no matter how loud I shouted. As I fell deeper and deeper into this hole, I lost any sense of myself. I was just following what everyone else was doing, just a doll in the grand scheme of things. I think the quote at the bottom sums up what was happening to me. "Why do so many ... settle for so little? I don't understand why they're not greedy for what's inside them." There was a lot inside of me, but I was hiding it so no one could see it, not even me.

Other Ideas for Sharing

Many books provide other great ideas to get your group started on telling their stories. (Consider, for example, Dan B. Allender's book, *To Be Told*, WaterBrook, 2006.) If you find a workbook that invites people to talk about their histories, try that. I use several workbooks I put together for this purpose (*Leave the Mud and Learn to Soar*, or *Come with Me*), which contain exercises and journaling questions people can do at home to then share with the group. But just about any good book can be useful if you find ways to engage with it personally.

This level of sharing is often a new experience for people and they're not sure how to do it. If you are leading a group, I would suggest you go first, telling your own story, sharing your timeline or genogram. This helps other members understand the kind of sharing you are looking for and it gives them permission to dive in. Heather, who directs a college ministry, started a new small group recently. She told me she started off the group by telling her own story, sharing how she'd been raped in high school. She said, "I was so surprised by the things they shared after I went first. I'd known these women for a while but they had never opened up about their own experiences until they heard me share mine."

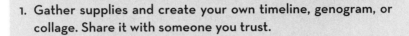

YOUR TURN

1. Gather supplies and create your own timeline, genogram, or collage. Share it with someone you trust.

2. Write about what you learned about yourself in the process of creating your story.

CHAPTER 4

How Does That Make You Feel?

Facing our anxiety about being real

"Here is a simple, rule-of-thumb guide for behavior: Ask yourself what you want people to do for you, then grab the initiative and do it for them. Add up God's Law and Prophets and this is what you get."

Matthew 7:12 (MSG)

My friend Dave is part of a group of men who are trying to get real with each other. In fact, they are so serious about it, they are using a workbook I wrote for women. These middle-aged guys have been believers for most of their lives but are still searching for deep relationships. I interviewed Dave about his experience:

Why did you want to do a group like this?

"Other groups I've been in were good. We got to share a lot about our lives, we got personal to a certain degree but [most of the time] it never really happened. We were trying to scratch at real authenticity but we never really did it. What we are doing now — the questions that are asked — is on a more personal level than I've ever experienced before in a men's group. We're sharing the story behind the story and talking about the whys and the mess-ups, the confessions, and we're putting stuff in the light."

How does it feel to be at that point now, of sharing the whole story?

"It can be scary. I don't know what's going to happen. They could misunderstand or judge me. Most of my life, through my mom, I've been judged, so I think I'm a little gun-shy. I'm afraid they might share things about me with others. I'm a cautious person. I have to push myself to take initiative in friendships, to go to other levels with friends. I didn't have that modeled but I understand the value. My tendency is to want to compare my story to the stories I've heard. I worry that I'll feel kind of embarrassed that I haven't had a really rotten life. I mean, there are some struggles that I've been through but I'm afraid of being evaluated by comparison. They might think, 'You don't have much of a story, David. There's really not much dirt. So what do you have to complain about? You shouldn't have any struggles. How come you're not more successful, grateful, or whatever.' But no one has reacted like that.

"I never had a dad that related to me on any sort of soul or spirit level. To interact with men on a deeper level is new. In the deepest sense, a meaningful relationship means I would be befriended by another man, and I would feel special to another man. I never felt special to my dad. It feels like this big empty hole."

How do you feel when other people share?

"I feel amazingly blessed that they trust me with something really personal to them. When one of the guys shared, I was just in awe. He's had a hard time and he was willing to tell it. All I could say was 'I'm sorry' and empathize. I felt like we took on or embraced his hurt somehow. I don't know if that's possible, but that's kind of how it felt to me, like in sharing, he was unloading a part of that because he wasn't carrying the whole thing by himself anymore."

How are you changing because of this?

"I take more initiative with my wife and my friends. Before, I thought I was weird because the only way I knew to relate was how I related to my dad—very informational, cerebral, about things we have in common, tasks, or activities. That's all I had to offer. I'm becoming more okay in who I am and what I value and what I can bring to this world. I even like a lot of who I am and I think some of that has come through acceptance from other men. After trust is developed, it creates a bond that is undefinable—it feels very spiritual, like there's some context for long-term interacting and friendship.

"I have felt more free to be honest with God too about me and my struggles. I argue with him more and just tell him stuff. Knowing that I'm not alone in how I think about God is really helpful."

SETTING THE STAGE FOR A SUCCESSFUL GROUP

Even though people volunteer to join a process group or sign up for a workshop or class, sometimes they become anxious as the sharing begins. This may happen to you too. If and when anxiety rears its head in the group, consider using the following suggestions for dealing with it:

1. Revisit the covenant.

Remind yourself and the group of your purpose. It's normal to feel anxious when you are doing something new. It's normal to wonder what people will think of you once they hear your story, to feel you are a bigger mess than others, to be afraid people will judge you, to wonder if this was a good idea after all. Talk about your fears together. It will be reassuring and bonding to hear others express the same concerns. Then, having jumped off this cliff won't seem quite so stupid.

Acknowledge that what we are doing here is likely very different than what we have done in small groups before. We are not giving intellectual answers to specific questions; we are talking about our lives and it's messy work. There's no easy seven-step formula to follow. We will learn together by trial and error. We will each make mistakes, say some stupid things, and perhaps inadvertently hurt each other. This is

2. Prepare for the question: "Is it really biblical to rehash the past?"

Being real with other people is thoroughly biblical. We are trying to apply our theology to our lives. We are trying to live out concepts such as confession, bearing one another's burdens, examining our hearts, walking in the light, and being transformed by the renewing of our minds. Look up Psalm 51:6–12, Galatians 6:2, James 5:16, and 1 John 1:5–10 for starters. Read *The Emotionally Healthy Church* by Peter Scazzero (Zondervan, 2003) and *Changes That Heal* by Dr. Henry Cloud (Zondervan mass paperback, 1997) for more help.

Sometimes people worry that talking about our histories is about blaming others or looking for sympathy. This is not our purpose. It's about telling the truth, exposing the facts to the light. Many pieces of our stories are hidden, tucked away in shame. Ignoring them only gives them power. Telling our stories allows us to explore how our wounds at the hands of others led to wounds of our own making. It shows us where we've hardened our hearts and become bitter and self-protective. Our hesitancy to attend to our own hearts and histories is not based on rational argument but on fear. People are clearly not better off, not more emotionally healthy, and certainly not more spiritually mature for having avoided dealing with their stuff. This process forces us to answer the question, "Can I face myself?" It's not a path for cowards; it's about a real renovation, about opening ourselves — who we are and who we have been — to God's healing, transforming power.

But I understand people's hesitation. It's a lot like a woman giving birth for the first time. In the middle of labor, you just want out. You wonder what you were thinking when you decided to do this. You didn't know it would be this hard or hurt this bad and you start screaming at the guy who got you into this mess, but eventually, excruciatingly, this beautiful thing emerges, clarifying everything and changing your whole life!

3. Talk frequently about how to respond to each other's stories.

Most of us respond to the pain of others in one of two ways — we either want to run or we shift to problem-solving/distracting strategies. Here's how it goes down. Someone shares something difficult: their spouse is cheating on them or they are struggling with alcohol addiction. The listeners get anxious. The news feels big. They don't know what to do. So some of them run for cover. They disengage and wander off somehow. They may remain physically present but they are no longer involved in the conversation. Others shift into overdrive. They are anxious too, but they cope by taking over. They start offering suggestions, "this is what you should do" kinds of statements. They have stopped listening and will likely miss any cues that they are not being helpful.

It's important to recognize that advising without being invited is about taking care of oneself instead of the other person. Shifting to fix-it mode means you don't have to sit with someone in their struggle. Instead of feeling sad or powerless or upset about what they are going through, you can focus on possible solutions. This keeps you safely in your own head and also gives you the false sense that you are doing something useful for the other person.

What does advice-giving truly accomplish anyway? How often does the other person actually feel helped? How often do they act on the advice? How often is the advice new information, something the person hasn't already thought of or tried? How often does it address the underlying issues that are causing the problem? When you are tempted to advise without being asked, remember what it feels like. Remember how often you've been annoyed, offended, even hurt by someone's premature, simplistic solution to your complex, painful situation. If we want our group to work, we have to train ourselves and our group members to do things differently:

- Talk about advice-giving tendencies in your group. Encourage members to identify what they tend to do when they hear about

the struggles of others. Just acknowledging our reactions out loud opens up the opportunity for change to begin.
- Talk about why. Discuss: What am I feeling when I do this? What am I trying to accomplish with my strategy? Am I trying to make the problem go away so I don't have to hear about it anymore? Is it about my need to feel good about myself by doing something to help? Am I uncomfortable because this issue is a struggle/experience I relate to?
- Talk about the effect of advice-giving. What is it like for you when someone disengages or tries to give advice.
- Develop a plan for your group. You might want to create a statement that your group will use to help each other deal with advice-giving. For example, "When we are tempted to give advice we will give ourselves a reality check. We will acknowledge that we are not here to fix each others' problems. We will remind ourselves that other people's problems are like our own. They are often long-term, complicated, and need to be solved by the person they belong to. Instead we will offer what we are looking for ourselves—validation and support."
- Point out to the group when advice-giving happens. Intervene immediately, but gently each time someone shifts to advice-giving. I try to keep it light by saying something like, "I know we really want to help Debbie right now and we have profound things to say, but I want to remind us of our promise to let everyone be in charge of their own life. Let's ask Debbie what she really needs from us right now."
- Give yourself and your group some grace. Advice-giving is a hard habit to break and it will take time.

4. Listen and validate.

Without the ability to give advice, group members may feel lost, so they should focus on what they can do: to listen and validate. This is your new mantra. Your group's goal is to help people feel heard and understood, to sit with each other as they share, not needing to solve or change anything in this moment, just accepting where others are in their journey.

Validating statements are responses like these:

- "I can see why you would feel like that."
- "Your feelings really make sense given what you've been through."
- "That sounds so difficult/painful/confusing."
- "I'm sorry you're going through that."

People worry that if they validate someone's feelings or experience, they are agreeing, in essence saying, "Yes, you should feel/react/think like that." They worry that if they try to understand, they will be endorsing bad behavior. They worry that people will stay stuck if they are not urged to move immediately. Actually, the opposite happens. When people don't feel validated, their feelings intensify. Because they don't feel understood, they may continue telling you the same information over again, hoping you'll get it the next time. Or they may abruptly stop talking because they can see you're not really trying to understand.

For those of us who are helpers, the idea of just listening and validating can sometimes feel like doing nothing. We have all this clever, profound stuff to pass on and we know it could totally change people's lives if they would just listen to us! So I say this lovingly and as a recovering advice-giver myself: "You're not helping!" You can see the truth of this clearly when you are the one being vulnerable. What is it you want? Do you want someone to tell you what to do, or give you some pat answer, or tie your problem up with a pretty little bow? What you're looking for is some understanding. You want to feel less alone, less crazy, and validating does that.

Validating also opens the door to change. When people feel heard, the intensity of their feelings begins to dissipate and they often experience renewed energy to move on to problem-solving strategies. Then they may ask for help in brainstorming new things to try, or support to follow through. The key is to wait for them to ask for it. When we get impatient and try to hurry things along, it tells people, "Your problem is too big for me. I need you to make it go away." Staying calm and listening communicates that you can handle what you're hearing and are not afraid or overwhelmed by it. This gives people strength and hope.

Even people who should know better forget this sometimes. Me, for example. The other evening I met with a client who's been dealing with depression. She had been improving lately and I expected her to be doing better, but she wasn't. I was tired after a week away from home and she was trying to tell me how depressing it was to be depressed, which of course it is. I did all the wrong things. I tried to talk her out of her feelings and then I minimized them too. I tried to tell her that everyone struggles with depression sometimes and that she is not a failure, and that we should focus on what she could do to help herself, blah, blah, blah. The more I tried to shift her focus, the more intense her feelings got. By the time it was over, I felt completely powerless to help her and she felt more depressed. As soon as she left, I saw my mistake. I called her the next day to see how she was and she told me she was mad, "You weren't very compassionate last night." She was right. And there was nothing to do then but apologize and tell her that next time I will let her feel what she is feeling.

During the last year of my master's program in marriage and family therapy, just before we began working with real clients, our professor gave us some final instructions. She addressed what we were all feeling—this huge sense of responsibility—would we understand the problems correctly, would we come up with the right interventions, would we be able to help people do better or would we make things worse? The professor said that during the first weeks of practicing therapy we should focus on one thing: "Just stay in the room and breathe."

So remind yourself and the rest of the group to relax, "stay in the room and breathe," and simply offer your presence. What other people are looking for is the same thing you are looking for. Someone who won't fall apart when they hear your story, and who will communicate in some way, "Your feelings make sense to me. I'm here for you."

5. Brace yourself for things to be messy and unfinished.

One of the difficulties of creating places for authenticity is that things will get a lot messier than when everyone is hiding and playing nice. You may be surprised by the amount of pain and struggle happening in the lives of people you've been doing church with for a long time. It may take a little getting used to—seeing people in this more holistic way—finding out that the efficient woman who runs your children's ministry was sexually violated as a child and still has regular nightmares, or that the cheerful guy who runs the sound board experiences anxiety attacks. Everybody's got a story. Everybody is dealing with something. But after we get over the shock of seeing all the pain, it can be such a relief, acknowledging what is already there.

Creating change takes a long time. Dealing with a childhood trauma or the betrayal of a loved one will take years. Changing negative beliefs and letting go of addictive behaviors will require a prolonged fight. We will need to learn to get comfortable with things taking time, and being a mess for a while. But as we model extending grace to others, they will learn to do the same for themselves and for us. And that will enable us all to grow.

6. Pay attention to the impact of sharing.

It's not just what is being talked about during group meetings that's important but what's happening while things are being shared. As you become more comfortable with the group process, be aware of what's going on in the other members as one person is sharing. Occasionally one person's sharing triggers big feelings in someone else. You might notice someone looking anxious or angry or close to tears. When the person speaking is finished, address what you see, "Linda, you look upset. What's going on with you?" This gives her the opportunity to explore how she is relating to what she's heard. She may say that she's had a similar experience or that someone she loves is going through that right now, or that she feels sad about what the sharer has gone through. Paying attention to how we are impacted by each other's stories provides natural openings for group members to connect with one another and deepen the level of intimacy.

Sometimes you'll notice negative group dynamics during meetings. For example, some members may be participating too much and others are shutting down. It's tempting to go to group members individually and talk about a particular issue, but as much as you can, keep conversations *about* the group happening *in* the group. Casually mention what you've noticed. "It seems that some of you are not sharing much. I'm wondering if we can talk about that." They may say they are not really relating to the discussion today, or that they are particularly tired today, or that they feel there isn't really time for them to share. Regardless of the reason, it allows the group to address problems as a group and come up with solutions together. It's best to bring up issues as soon as you notice them, before people begin to feel resentful or talk about each other outside of the group.

There will be conflict in any group. This is okay. It can be an indicator that something good is going on — people are buying in enough to care, to need something from each other. Talk about the fact that sometimes we might feel uncomfortable with each other and it's important to talk about it. This is all part of building community and we don't need to be afraid of it. We want to continually communicate that responsibility for the group belongs to the group. We share ownership. Succeed or fail, we do it together.

7. Check in with group members periodically.

Evaluating the group from time to time not only helps us assess whether we are moving in the right direction but also teaches group members to think about and ask for what they need. Discuss these questions as a group:

- Are you feeling heard, safe?
- Are you learning new things about yourself?
- Are you experiencing growth?
- Are there some things you would like from the group that you are not getting?

PROBLEMS IN SMALL GROUP SETTINGS

As alluded to earlier, process groups are not without their occasional problems. That's just inevitable. Try not to panic or let the group fall apart. Just do your best to tackle the issues and keep moving forward. Following are some of the common issues you might face.

People Who Talk Too Much

It's important to deal with dominating personalities as soon as you see a pattern developing. Certainly there will be weeks when the focus is on a few people because of a crisis or difficult struggle, but if someone continually dominates, you need to address it. Remind the group at the beginning of the meeting to make time for everyone to share. If that doesn't work, when there's a break in the talkative person's flow, direct your attention to the group and ask, "What about others of you? Do you relate? What do you think about this issue?" This helps communicate to the dominating person, in an indirect way, that their turn is over and reminds them that others need the opportunity to share. Another strategy is to sit next to the talkative person and slow them down with a hand on their arm or leg and say directly to them, "Let's see how others are doing."

If neither of these approaches works after several attempts, you may be dealing with someone who isn't able to function well in a group setting. Consider addressing the matter during group—a difficult conversation, for sure, but one potentially very useful to the dominating person. Invite others to share, kindly and respectfully of course, when this person dominates. The person may just not realize what they are doing and will adjust when confronted. If, however, the person isn't able or willing to change their behavior, help them exit the group as gracefully as possible. "It looks like this isn't a good fit for you right now. I'm suggesting that you try _____ instead." Screening potential group members up front may help avoid this situation, but if a mistake has been made, just correct it and move on. Not everyone can do this kind of group. (Refer to chapter 7 on dealing with difficult people.)

People Who Are Upset with Other Group Members

It's not unusual for some group members to complain to the leader about someone or something in the group. This does not mean that something's wrong with your group. Deal with issues that are affecting the group as a group. For example, a couple of members continually come late to group, to the growing frustration of the rest. Tell your group that an issue has come up that needs discussion and resolution. First, reassure them that while nobody likes conflict, it's a normal and inevitable part of significant relationships, an opportunity for everyone to learn to better care for one another. Then ask those who have a concern to express it. This is where things can get ugly if you as facilitator don't stay involved. Help those who have a concern to think through what they want to say and how they can lovingly express it. Ask them to look underneath their anger. What else are they feeling? Usually anger covers a more vulnerable feeling such as embarrassment, fear, or hurt. Perhaps their concern could be expressing something like this, "When people come late, I find myself feeling anxious. I'm afraid that maybe they don't really want to do this process with me and then I shut down." (You could read this example to the group to give them a sense of how to express their concerns.) Keep the complaint focused on how the person sharing is feeling rather than the behavior they are upset about. Using general terms rather than "you" softens the confrontation and helps those hearing it to be less defensive.

People Who Are in a Crisis

A person in the throes of a crisis provides an opportunity to create some real intimacy in your group. The person in crisis (marriage falling apart, loss of a loved one, struggling child, discovery of cancer, whatever) will need all of you to help carry the burden they are experiencing. It's okay to spend more time on this person for a period of time, perhaps several weeks. Try to help the group clarify what they can and can't do to help. There may be practical assistance they can offer outside of group time, for example, providing meals or babysitting, or making phone calls. Be careful that the crisis doesn't become the only issue the group is dealing with. Over time such an imbalance will cause other group members to feel that their issues are not important and the group may begin to fall apart.

People Who Are Stuck in Major Sin

Let's say someone in your group reveals that they are currently having an affair or getting drunk several times a week. When people feel safe, they will reveal all kinds of things. The fact that they have done so means your group is really working, so don't get freaked out. Remember, stay in the room and breathe. It's not your job to fix this. Our goal is to support people in their journey with God, not to take over when they are not doing well. Fortunately, when someone shares something like this, they are generally looking for a way out and some help to make the move. Focus on asking questions, exploring why they are involved in this behavior. Ask what needs the behavior meets for them, what they are really looking for. Then help them talk about the consequences of this behavior in their life and what they need in order to let go of it. Encourage the group to express their concern for the person and their hope for restoration but interrupt anything that sounds shaming, judging, or controlling. One of the hard lessons you learn as a therapist is that people are going to do what they are going to do. Expressing disapproval or anger about bad behavior is not going to make it *stop*; it will only make people *stop talking* about it. Then the issues go underground and we've lost our opportunity to help create change.

As with a crisis, don't get stuck on it. Everyone is struggling with some issue and needs the opportunity to explore it. The group's purpose is to help each person move further along on their journey, whatever their spiritual condition.

We learned this through trial and error in one of our first groups years ago, when a woman shared that she was having an affair. Our group certainly made some mistakes in our efforts to help her, but she has often said that our commitment to accept and love her in the middle of her struggle was what gave her the strength to walk away from it. She has been running groups ever since and many women would say their lives are transformed today because of the way she has extended grace to them.

People Who Are Emotionally Shut Down or Who Intellectualize Everything

Sometimes people think they want to be in a process group but when they see what it really involves, they go into hiding. They aren't used to talking about their feelings and it's terrifying for them. Creating safety in the group is especially important for such a person. Their coping mechanism is there for a reason. They hide because they've been hurt in the past and will need to be wooed out of their head and into their heart.

While they may not have access to many feelings, most people can at least identify with anger. It may be the only feeling they are aware of. Someone who's more in tune emotionally will recognize shame or guilt or hurt or rejection, but someone who's very shut down will interpret all of these as anger. Anger is a secondary emotion; it comes as a defense mechanism to protect against some kind of hurt, to avoid feeling vulnerable to that hurt again.

If anger is all a person's got, start with that. When they tell their stories, ask exploring questions: "What was that like for you? How did it make you feel?" Invite them to talk about situations or relationships in which they have experienced anger, then ask them to consider what other feeling might be underneath the anger. Suggest some possibilities, "I wonder if maybe you were also feeling embarrassed (rejected, ignored, etc.) when that happened?"

It's important not to ignore a shut-down person because aside from missing out on her own growth, she will affect the other group members. Someone living in her head may not be comfortable with others revealing deep feelings and may attempt to stop them from sharing by giving advice or showing subtle disapproval. This dynamic can keep an entire group from feeling safe enough to accomplish its goals.

When someone remains in a self-protective shell for a long time, it may be best to discuss with them whether this kind of group is really what they are looking for. Give people permission to leave the group by saying, "It's okay if this isn't a fit for you right now. Maybe you need something different, perhaps a Bible study or a class. We want you to be where you can grow and if this group isn't it, that's okay." Sometimes people who find a process group overwhelming the first time around will return years later to try again when they are more ready.

People Who Don't Want to Change

We can get all wrapped up in what somebody needs to do to get better, but if they don't want it for themselves, it's just not going to happen. The group of therapists I work with regularly consults on cases, and one of the things we often ask each other when one of us is upset about a client's lack of progress is, "Are you working harder than your client?" Helpers need to remind each other that no matter how much we care or how hard we work, ultimately, whether people change or not is up to them. They have to want it for themselves and they have to do the work. If we get too involved, we will not only waste our energy but we may stand in the way of someone learning to take responsibility for their own life.

ENDING A SUCCESSFUL GROUP

Sometimes groups will carry on for years. Some members may leave while new ones join but the core of the group keeps going. One of the groups my girlfriends and I started more than ten years ago is still meeting weekly. This is a beautiful thing when it happens but often groups will end for some reason — the series or book is finished, too many members can't continue, people want to try something new. Whatever the reason, honor what has gone on in the group by spending some time talking about what you experienced together. Here are some ideas:

- Ask each person to share how they are feeling about the group ending — sad, anxious, ready, etc.
- Write cards or letters of encouragement about how each member has touched your life. Read these aloud, then give them to each other to keep.

- Pray together for each person, specially addressing that person's ongoing needs or celebrating growth that has occurred.
- Plan a party for your last meeting and just have fun together.
- If possible, make plans to get together periodically to reconnect. Hopefully many of the relationships will continue outside of group anyway.

These are also good ideas if a number of people are leaving at the same time, or if someone is leaving to lead another group. Having a send-off for this person will empower them as they begin the hard work of creating a new process group.

I am always amazed at the power of a group. They can do things for each other I can never do in a therapy setting. Nothing beats what happens when someone steps out and shares a painful story or shameful secret and then watches a roomful of people nod and express understanding and acceptance. That's God's love in action. And it's life changing!

YOUR TURN

1. What's your emotional reaction when people share something painful? Why do you think you react as you do?

2. Are some issues more difficult for you to hear about than others? What are they? Any ideas about why that is?

3. What emotions in others are most difficult for you to tolerate? Anger? Sadness? Hopelessness? Fear?

4. What emotions were acceptable in your family of origin? What emotions were unacceptable?

Chapter 5

Group Therapy for the Masses

Reimagining Sunday mornings

> The righteous cry out, and the LORD hears them; he delivers them from all their troubles. The LORD is close to the brokenhearted and saves those who are crushed in spirit.
>
> Psalm 34:17 – 18

Creating experiences that allow for authentic sharing on Sunday mornings (or whenever you have your large service) is a daunting task. Not because it's hard to do but because people aren't expecting it. They are used to coming to church to observe, not participate. Sure, you've got a few folks who come with pen and paper, eager to learn something new, but most of the gang will be halfway checked out soon after the singing and announcements are over.

I feel your pain. Occasionally my pastor asks me to take a Sunday morning service for him. Usually I say no. It's not that I mind teaching, it's just that it's a pretty tough gig. The last time he asked me, he did this underhanded, manipulative thing—wrote me a clever note about my brilliance and something about laying prostrate at my feet, begging. I'm a sucker for a cleverly crafted note, and the image of my pastor begging was more than I could take, so I said yes. But once I'm standing there, I find the whole thing surreal. I'm used to people really engaging, to an interactive dialogue about significant issues, so I'm just not sure what to do with a roomful of people passively staring at me. I feel so isolated I start to get anxious. "What am I doing here?" I always think. So I start telling self-deprecating stories, hoping people will laugh so I will feel less alone. It's all the more agonizing for me because I know many of these people, or at least people like them — folks who are struggling in their marriages, with their kids, with depression, illness, anxiety, addictions — and it's all I can do not to say, "Can we just stop playing this church game and talk to each other about what's really going on?"

But just because people are used to being left alone doesn't mean we shouldn't try something different. For all the reasons we've already talked about, we have got to give it a shot and see if over time, through trial and error, we can change the culture of our communities.

LIFE AT THE REFUGE

Kathy Escobar and Karl Wheeler, who copastor a community of about 150 people in Colorado, are all about shaking things up. Both Kathy and Karl were on staff at a mega church when they became disillusioned with the system. They and their spouses began dreaming together about a different kind of church and out of that created a unique faith community they call the Refuge. One of their stated values is to embrace brokenness, their own as well as their members'. They believe that regular confession ought to be a way of life for everyone in the church, especially those in leadership, and they design opportunities for it to happen. They believe in dialogue, in letting people speak. The focus isn't up front, on the professionals. It's interactive. Here's a little of their experience so far:

> *When we planted the Refuge fifteen months ago, there were many people who thought (and secretly hoped) we'd replicate the "attractional" church model that we had been part of. It could have been so simple — a few good messages; amazing, upbeat music; a few light trees and fog machines; and we would have been golden. One good communicator and one solid care pastor, it was the formula for success. One problem — it violated so many of our core beliefs about what "church" is supposed to be. So instead we have chosen this harder path in the wider Christian community. At this point we aren't sure if we're smart or stupid.*

Planting a church is hard. Planting a church that is committed to trying wacky things is harder. Planting a church that is committed to being safe for wacky people (as in every human being, when we're really honest) is even harder. The reason we have chosen the harder path is that we believe simply and firmly in grace. Not theoretical grace. Not grace when it works in our favor. Not grace that is just a nice Christian word. To us, grace means cutting each other a lot of slack, offering a ton of mercy and understanding instead of judgment.

We're not saying that there's not a lot of grace offered out there in the wider Christian community. Of course there is, but in the average church there's not a ton of need for a lot of it to be dispensed. Really, people's craziness isn't rubbing against each other too much. You pass out bulletins, you sit, you listen, you go home. You might need to give grace to the guy who stole your parking spot or the person in front of you who decided to talk to his wife during the worship, but the truth is that for the most part, real grace isn't necessary.

But that all changes when you really share your lives together in community. When you show up on Sunday, open the floor, and give room for comments and thoughts from all over the place. When even the people in "leadership" don't hide but say their crazy thoughts out loud. When there's not a program to hide behind but just this raw, real authentic entrance into the messiness of life. When people feel safe enough to share really deep things out loud.

What we have done that is most unique is create a conversational style. It took time to do, it didn't happen right away. We sort of eased into it and modeled safety by sharing our own struggles pretty honestly at first, then getting a few other people to share theirs, and then over time we created a culture where every week people participate in some way. The teaching is always interactive, in fact we don't teach in the traditional sense. We "teach" by facilitating the conversation, opening it up to people sharing their hearts, asking questions. We don't really "control" the conversation in that all are welcome to participate. Sometimes it's scary and we have to redirect things but on the whole, nothing is orchestrated or programmed. We do a lot of whiteboarding together, brainstorming, writing, reflective time, moving around, drawing, etc. We also created a blog so we could just talk with each other. We never really edit too much, we shoot straight about our struggles with believing God, loving him, loving ourselves, loving our neighbor. We don't have an us-them mentality. We are all in this together.

Our leadership team is not really focused on budgets and strategies (we hate that word) but rather a culture of honesty. When our team meets there are always check-ins, what is going on in people's hearts, men and women together sharing life. We have five women and five men on our team. Every week someone cries and it's not always the women, for sure. It really is beautiful.

When Kathy and Karl talk about what they are doing, you can always hear a mixture of excitement and fear. They are doing something they have never seen modeled before. This is not something seminary equipped them to do and yet they feel strongly that it's what God is calling them to. I don't know specifically what God is calling you to and I don't want to suggest that it ought to look exactly like the Refuge, but I can't help feeling that this is a little closer to what Jesus has in mind for his church. If you want to move a little in that direction, here are some ideas you could try or use as inspiration from the Refuge. You can check them out at *www.therefugeonline.org*.

IDEAS FROM THE REFUGE
1. Confessional Night

In this meeting attendees focused in on 1 John 1:9: "If we confess our sins, he is faithful and just and will forgive us our sins and purify us from all unrighteousness," as well as James 5:16, "Therefore confess your sins to each other and pray for each other so that you may be healed."

The stage was set with three stools and three individuals came up to share about a sin in their lives. Kathy prepared the group for the confessions by talking about why they were doing it (to live out the Scripture), and how important it was to listen well and to treasure what was being shared. People were asked to respect the courage it takes to confess sin publicly and not to tell others about the personal things they were about to hear that night. Then each of the three individuals spoke, with Karl speaking last. They talked again about confidentiality and protecting the sacredness of such honesty. Then they prepared the whole group to participate in confession by discussing the need to let out things that are eating at us rather than keeping them in.

Each person was given a washable marker and asked, if willing, to write on their hand(s) anything they wanted to confess at that moment: something they were struggling with presently, something from the past, whatever came to mind. During this time, music was played as well as a video produced by Paul Romig-Leavitt. (See the video at *www.confess.therefugeonline.org* or *www.torncurtainarts.org*.) Then everyone was invited to come forward, where leaders had set up four wash basins on tables (just white bowls with soap and rags), with two women or two men at each bowl (so people could go to whomever they felt more comfortable). People could choose whether or not to show the writing on their hands to the folks at the bowls, who would then ask, "Can we wash your hands?" Then they gently washed off whatever had been written on their hands and dried them.

Beyond that, a table was set up with a display of Bible verses about sins being washed away, lots of candles, and the communion elements. If people so desired, they could take communion before returning to their seats.

2. The Lord's Prayer

In this service, the Lord's Prayer was separated into phrases and displayed, one by one, on PowerPoint for meditation. (I've included only the interactive pieces.)

"Our Father who is in heaven." Kathy talked about how hard it is for some of us to be comforted by the word "father" because our own fathers were absent or rejecting or abusive. Those relationships have created distortions in the way we view God and how we expect him to deal with us. People were then asked to spend some time thinking, writing, talking about what God would be like if he were a really good father (which of course he is). What would he do, what would he say, how would it feel to be around him?

"Forgive us our debts, as we also have forgiven our debtors." Leaders placed candles on tables and asked people to light a candle for anyone they needed to forgive or something they needed forgiveness for.

"And lead us not into temptation but deliver us from evil." Everyone was given a slip of paper that said, "God, right now I really want to . . . ," asked to fill out whatever they were tempted by, and then the papers were collected. Then four people stood in the back and took turns reading them out loud. (When Kathy told me about this she said, "Oh my gosh, they were crazy honest, like 'go look at porn,' 'hurt myself,' 'eat,' etc. I got one that said 'masturbate' and I had to say it out loud in church! It was wild but I think it really helped shape our culture." The service ended with communion and a time of worship.

3. Love Letters

During a series on sex, one of the leadership team members shared about being a single woman who hasn't yet had sex. She shared how hard that has been but also how she is learning to experience intimacy with people in other ways. She read Song of Solomon. Then she asked everyone to write a brief love letter to whomever they wanted to write — to God, their spouse, boyfriend, girlfriend, whomever. Then she asked volunteers to read their letter aloud.

4. Safety Seat

The idea of the safety seat came from Karl. He knew someone who had a seat in his house designated as the "safety seat." When the kids sat in it, they could say absolutely anything with no consequence. "What," Karl asked those at the Refuge, "if we could tell God absolutely anything we wanted with no consequence? Would anyone like to give it a try?" Several people did. They were encouraged to be as honest as they could and to say it to God, not to the group. Here is Kathy's report of a few of the responses:

"A single mom, with a little kid — she looks up and says, 'God, I love you, I believe in you, you have redeemed so many things in my life and I am grateful, but I am now seeing my son go through some of the things that happened to me and I am just telling you right now, don't f___ with him!'

"A precious woman, dealing with bipolar mood disorder: 'God, I do believe, but I just want to tell you, I am so sick of how hard you make things. Are you ever going to give me a break?'

"A dad, average guy, white suburban professional: 'God, I am doing everything I know how to do to connect with you but I am pretty p___ off that I don't hear from you too much. I don't know what else to do, really. I'm here, I'm working as hard as I can to develop a relationship with you but it feels one-sided.'

"It honestly was one of the most amazing times I have ever experienced in church."

Other Ideas

An alternative form of the love letter idea is the letter of lament, in which you can encourage people to write about loss, disappointment or despair, frustration or rage. You might help them get started by reading one of David's lamenting psalms and talking about his example of an authentic relationship with God, one that includes conversations that are both joyful and painful.

Similar to the idea of completing the sentence about temptation, you might try one of the following:

- "Right now I'm really sad about ..."
- "I get discouraged when ..."
- "I lost something precious when ..."

Or you could try letters of gratitude:

- "I experience joy when ..."
- "My life feels abundant when ..."
- "I am so thankful for ..."

Or, talk about how to minister to one another as a community when a need arises, writing down on a whiteboard people's thoughts to such questions as:

- "When I have a burden that's too heavy to bear, I want people to …"
- "When I'm in pain, the last thing I want is … "
- "Things that people do to help that are not actually helpful are …"
- "Things that have meant a lot to me during a hard time are …"

LIFE AT FLOOD

I also interviewed Leeana Tankersley, a staff member at Flood church in San Diego, an emergent congregation of about 1,600. The staff at Flood values authenticity and are trying to create a community that not only believes in emotional health but lives it out.

What makes it hard to create experiences that lead your congregation toward emotional health?

"Our brokenness as leaders, to put it simply. We all have our own ways of resisting authenticity, of hiding our true selves—isolating ourselves, trying harder, creating busyness to feed our need for significance. When the people who are leading have underground issues, that creates a barrier right there. It's scary because if we are going to do this, we are going to have to deal with our own stuff. For some, it's just not a part of what they've done before. So there's resistance. I hear, 'Do we really need to do that? It's fluffy, emotional. Where does the Bible teaching come in? Jesus didn't sit around and talk about his past or his feelings all the time. He went out and did the work. We're wasting time sitting around, hashing and rehashing our issues.' Convenient how we forget that he was God and we are slightly less lucky! And sure, there is such a thing as 'paralysis from analysis,' but I believe it's an open, honest, healing community that best prepares us to 'do the work' of our Father.

"Then from some of the congregation, when we are not doing line-by-line expository teaching, we get, 'You're heretical.' It's a big thing to fight against. And they don't leave. They just complain. Some people are stuck on the overarching importance of propositional truth and often neglect the importance that Christ himself put on holistic ministry. We are trying to help people understand that propositional truth is not transformational in and of itself. We believe that transformation happens in a variety of ways, not just through teaching."

So how do you deal with that?
"Well, first of all (and all the church staff members and leaders will understand what I mean here), you try not to lose your mind with weariness and sarcasm. You allow people to be on a journey with this stuff and you decide you're going to walk with them as so many have walked with you. You decide you're not going to treat people like they're fools. Instead you're going to be gentle. But that's only possible on the days when you're feeling really good about yourself, your hair, and your marriage! The other days of the week, you have to pray that God will show you how to lead as you follow him. You pray, 'God, I want to be really argumentative and defensive with this person who is totally missing it. In fact, I basically feel like I'm more spiritually enlightened than he/she is. But God, please don't let me treat them that way.' That's the personal component. And I think there's a corporate component as well.

"You have to get clear about your values. You have to decide, as a staff first and then with your community of leadership, what your church is going to be about. We went on this journey as a church recently—clarifying our values, trying to define what God is calling this church to be, not what's the latest popular thing, but where God is giving us favor. We want to be true to that. We wrestled as a staff. We talked through all the things that are important to us and distilled the list down to a few words that we felt really communicated what makes Flood church different from the church down the street.

"But we didn't just come up with this list of cool-sounding words. We put legs to them. We can't just throw out these terms like 'postmodern church' if nobody knows what they mean. So we described what a community marked by these values would look like, what the people in this kind of church would do, and who they would be. Once we had workshopped this thing for months, our entire staff signed the paper in blood (well, not really, but you get what I mean . . . we all agreed that this was it for us). And then we took it to our volunteer leadership at our church—our 'crew'—and we met for five Sundays over the summer and got their input, feedback, ideas, pushback, etc. And we tweaked things and then we brought them to the entire church in our fall series. This was painstaking, just to be honest. But highly worth it. Hopefully, by now, people know what makes Flood church unique. They know what to expect of the community and what the community expects of them. If people are looking for a place where they can come and spectate, Flood church is not the place for them. We need participants. We need people who are bringing their whole selves to our church and participating even if they don't do it perfectly, especially if they don't do it perfectly.

"Since we are clear about our identity, we can allow people to be a part of that or choose not to be. When people get frustrated, we point them to our values and say, 'This is what we are about.' We have no problem saying to them, 'Sounds like the values you are looking for in a church are not the values we have here. There are great churches out there and it would really be better for you if you went to a church that matches your values.' We're not afraid to let people go if that's what needs to happen. And sometimes it does."

What would you say to that church leader who is trying to bring more authenticity to their community?

"So many leaders find it nearly impossible to change the tide of their church, to change the culture and the values. It feels like an uphill battle, like you're defeated before you've even begun. But, I can tell you, it's worth the journey. If you want to be a church that values authentic community, emotional health, holistic ministry, and you're needing to convince some people in your church, I have a great word for you. One of my very smart coworkers, Scott, shared this with our staff during our process of clarifying and communicating our values. He said, 'How do you turn an aircraft carrier? Steady pressure on the rudder.'

"We also have to do some myth busting about what it means to be a leader. To confront this idea, 'I'm the leader, I don't have any problems. That's why they chose me.' We need to help staff think through not just what they are trying to create in their people but who they want to be themselves. Our church won't be safe if the people facilitating aren't aware of what it means for them personally to be holy, transformed, righteous.

"I think it would be great to have some of the staff ask on a Sunday morning, 'What do you expect of your leaders?' and then have those leaders talk about the dilemma of needing to be all that and knowing that they're not. To let them say, 'I'm struggling just like you are. Can I tell you that? Can I tell you I'm struggling, and still lead?'

"If you aren't on that journey yourself, it's a ruse and you know that deep down in your heart and that's why you burn out. You know that you're faking it, trying to keep up appearances. Take David for example. What a wreck! But God uses people who are a wreck."

I hear about this dilemma all the time from clients who are in leadership: "Should I be leading if I'm struggling?" The reality is that everyone is struggling in some way. Obviously if someone's out of control or not honestly facing their issues, they're in no shape to lead but the vast majority of folks in therapy are actively engaged in dealing with their stuff and trying to improve their relationships. My response to them is, "Of course you should. You're exactly the person who should be leading because you're aware, you're in the fight, and you understand what it takes to change. You're a great example of someone making their theology real in their life."

IDEAS FROM FLOOD

Flood does something they call a "Graffiti Wall." They put pieces of butcher paper all along the walls, tape it down to tables with duct tape, and lay markers around. There are prompts on the screen for people to respond to. The band leads through worship songs. People come up and write or draw their thoughts. For example, while talking about King David and his authentic spirituality, people were asked to respond by owning things about themselves. The prompt said, "I am ... I am not ...." People wrote things like:

- I am ... impatient
- I am not ... good when I am tired
- I am ... creative
- I am not ... focused
- I am not ... who my mother-in-law thinks I am
- I am not ... my sister
- I am ... lonely

The graffiti wall can be done with all kinds of topics. Just create a statement that people can respond to, such as:

- An attribute of God that is really important to you right now and why
- A dream you have
- A struggle you are going through
- A relationship you want to see change
- Something you are asking God for
- A fruit of the Spirit you want to develop
- A loss you are grieving
- A fear that is burdening you

You also might consider variations to the basic format. For example, you might begin the activity with the lights low. Then, as people become more comfortable with participating, turn the lights up and ask them to look around to see what others have written. Or, have people walk around the room afterward and touch someone else's words or drawings and pray for them, either aloud or silently. Or, if you have a smaller space and it's difficult for everyone to move around, have people call out their answers to a designated person who writes them all down.

Leeana also shared Flood's approach to communion: "We try to make communion interactive. We do it 'family style.' We have six-foot banquet tables around the room. There's a staff person at each table. When the table is filled, everyone takes communion together, then joins hands for prayer. We like doing it this way because in a large church with a lot going on, it's sometimes hard to connect with a lot of our community. This is a good opportunity for us as staff to have contact—to look people in the eye, to put a hand on their shoulder and pray together in small groups. The way people look at us tells us they are hurting and longing for contact."

In my own church, people are served communion in groups of ten or so by two servers. One server brings the bread and another the cup and serves each person individually. As they do, they look right at each person and say something, using their name whenever possible. It might be something as traditional as, "Karen, this is Christ's body given for you," or something more personal or relevant to the message that day, such as, "Sarah, you are so special to him he gave himself for you," "Mike, he is always watching over you, ready to rescue you," or "Sam, you are his precious child, he will never abandon you." Obviously, personalizing the experience may not be possible in a larger church, but when it is, it's a beautiful way to connect people to both the person serving them and to God.

Creating interactive large group worship experiences may be the scariest thing you will do. You will have little control over what happens. In a large group there are many variables: people you may not know well, people who like attention, people who are struggling with big issues. Prepare for things to get a little messy. Give yourself permission to take some time to figure it out, to make mistakes, to learn through trial and error. The upside is that you will be authentic and that's a step in the right direction.

YOUR TURN

1. What do you imagine might happen in your community if you tried one of these activities? What scares you or excites you about it?

2. What resistance might you encounter from others in leadership or from yourself?

> Let's pause from thinking about bringing more authenticity to your church community and concentrate on what pursuing authenticity will be like for you personally. Chapter 6 is an opportunity for you to consider this as well as how your own personal style of leadership might work for or against you. And because I'll ask you to do some self-evaluation during the course of the chapter, there won't be a "Your Turn" exercise at the end.

Chapter 6
Defense Mechanisms Galore
Leading from an authentic place

Keep vigilant watch over your heart; *that's* where life starts.

Proverbs 4:23 (MSG)

I am at the hospital with my daughter for an appointment when I see Marshall from my church. Marshall is in his eighties. He and his wife, Elizabeth, are deeply loved by our congregation. Marshall is what old men are supposed to be — calm and loving, wise and strong, with this look in his eye that tells you he's up to something. He spent most of his life as a school principal and, after retirement, mentored prison inmates, taking some into his home. Until a few years ago, he was an elder at our church and played in a jazz band with a bunch of kick-butt old guys. Then Elizabeth was diagnosed with Alzheimer's, and because Marshall is her caregiver, we've seen less and less of them.

Now Elizabeth also has cancer and is slowly, painfully dying. Marshall walks with two canes, also new in the last few years. He needs a hip replacement which is why he's at the hospital. He's looking much older these days. We talk for a few minutes and he tells me he misses everyone, but Elizabeth needs constant care and he can't leave her. His eyes are red and wet and sad. I'm afraid I will cry. Because Marshall is real, I can feel his pain easily. And his authenticity makes me aware of my inadequacy. I have nothing to offer worthy of his pain and honesty. No words to ease the daily torture of losing his love and his life. All I can do is hug him and whisper, "I'm so sorry." But then I can't shake him for days. His face is still there. His pain is still there. And I still feel inadequate.

I don't like that. I've spent way too much time in school to be standing here with nothing significant to offer. It's tempting to try to say something "pastoral" so that I can feel better and he can stop being devastated but instead there is only rawness.

Some days all this authenticity is too much and I want to go back to doing ministry the way I used to do it, before I got so involved. Back to when people's problems were tasks on my to-do list, when I didn't notice how much pain people were in and all I saw were behavior issues. Now, sometimes the pain is overwhelming. I have trouble carrying all the stories and secrets. I want what I offer to make a big difference... but sometimes it doesn't. Sometimes there's little relief as people struggle to bear deep sorrows or move agonizingly slowly toward recovery. And there's nothing for helpers to do but sit with them.

As much as I feel called to what I do, some days I just want to lock my doors and change my phone message to say, "I'm sorry, I will only be responding to your pain on Tuesday and Thursday from 10 to 2. If you have a difficulty at any other time, please call the crisis hotline. Thank you and have a nice day." Some days I am a coward. I want to do my work on autopilot, show up like a superhero, drop my pearls of wisdom, and then hightail it out of there before I get blood on me.

But I did that for a long time — offering people intellectual responses to their complex situations — and nothing much came of it. As I look back, I can see how self-protective it was. Focusing on the problems of others can easily become an escape from dealing with our own, protecting ourselves from things that need addressing in our own lives. We stay in our heads, disconnected from our hearts and approach our work from a one-up position — as problem solvers, experts, advisors, answer people. People who give help but don't need it.

OVERFUNCTIONERS

In her book, *The Dance of Anger*, Harriet Lerner says that people often get stuck functioning in certain roles in relationships and may have a hard time adjusting even when their strategy is not useful to themselves or others. She describes many of us in church leadership and helper roles when she talks about overfunctioners.[4]

Here's an example of what overfunctioning looks like. Kay served in the church for many years in lay ministry and then professionally as an associate and interim senior pastor. She's caring and brilliant and often says things that are so profound you want to write them down. But Kay is also deeply wounded—adopted as a baby by a woman who should have never been allowed to have children. She fell apart a few years ago when the weight of her history caught up with her, causing debilitating anxiety and depression. She's done a lot of work since then, facing and examining her story. We talked about her time as an associate pastor:

What was being in ministry like for you?

"Ministry was for me a total escape from brokenness. Like most people, I came from a dysfunctional family and life in the church didn't address how to deal with being broken and I don't even think I knew that I was broken. In the early '80s when I dedicated my life to Christ, there wasn't even a language of brokenness."

Did you feel you were hiding?

"I couldn't have said then that I was in pain. I was, but I couldn't identify that. I had already established a pattern of performance. On one hand, I never let people close but I wouldn't have known that because in my family we weren't close, it was so disconnected. I had no understanding of what that looked like or that you were supposed to do that. On the other hand, I was always transparent about what was going on with me. I remember starting at my professional job, and going in to talk to my boss (senior pastor) and sharing some pretty personal stuff but his response told me right away that he was not someone to share this stuff with. His response told me that he didn't know a lot about the world of the heart, so don't go there. I look back now and realize that was right about the time he began an affair, so that could have had something to do with it. I don't think I was far enough along then to realize how impoverished he was. But I've seen that over and over again. People who are just performing ministry machines, but something's not happening for them and they just implode.

"Growing in this stuff (emotional health) really is like a sunrise, slowly things are illuminated. At that time, I wasn't aware that I wasn't okay. I was a new minister. I finally got my dream. I think the fact that I achieved this ministry dream, the pinnacle of success, caused some of my needs to go underground. I'm performing my little heart out and getting tons of accolades because I'm very good at this, then the bottom drops out of this church when the pastor reveals he's leaving his wife and his ministry for this woman he's having an affair with. For a person like me, growing up in an alcoholic home, where any crazy thing can happen, I just went into survival mode. This is something I'm kind of used to. The feelings go numb and I just take care of business. I did a really good job taking care of that and got more accolades."

Another senior pastor was hired and became Kay's new boss. Unfortunately, Kay soon detected that the new pastor had ethical problems. She communicated her concerns to the elders but the pastor was never confronted. Eventually, she felt her only option was to quit.

What was going on emotionally after you left the church?

"I'm a slow cooker. I had a delayed reaction. I remained fairly shut down and numbed out. The church didn't make any efforts to place me anywhere. I tried to find another ministry job but eventually gave up. The trigger point came when I tried dating. Being in a relationship with a guy brought all the junk to the surface. I also experienced another ministry failure. I had joined a church community and had been asked to take over a dying ministry from someone else. It was inevitable that it would crumble but it felt like whatever I put my hand to died. As I became more aware emotionally, [the pain] manifested physically. I had a meltdown. The only way I can describe it is that I lost the ability to function.

My mind had always been my strength but something snapped upstairs. I couldn't do things that were second nature—reasoning and judgment were gone. I couldn't complete tasks, or make decisions, I couldn't drive for a while. And the church just dropped out of the picture—no phone calls or support. It was really a case of leaving your wounded to die. I wanted to yell, 'I'm sorry I can't put on a show for you, I'm falling apart.' Ministry was my identity. I'm still trying to find my way back from that time ten years ago. I'm still struggling to find a place."

What about you? Do any of the general themes of Kay's story describe you? Answer the following questions as you think about your style.

1. **Check any of the characteristics of overfunctioners that apply to you:**

    ☐ Know what's best not only for themselves but for others.

    ☐ Move in quickly to advise, rescue, and take over when stress hits.

    ☐ Have difficulty allowing others to struggle with their own problems.

    ☐ Avoid worrying about their own personal goals and problems by focusing on others.

    ☐ Have difficulty sharing their own vulnerable sides, especially with those people who are viewed as having problems.

    ☐ May be labeled the person who is "always reliable" or "always together."

2. **On a scale of 0–5 (0 = not concerned at all, 5 = totally terrified), how comfortable are you with people knowing the real you? Explain your answer.**

    _____
    _____
    _____
    _____

3. What fears do you have of sharing your struggles with others in your community?

_____
_____
_____
_____

4. What has happened in the past when you have shared?

_____
_____
_____
_____

UNDERFUNCTIONERS

Harriet Lerner also describes the partner to overfunctioner, the underfunctioner, which is what many of us are afraid we will become if we stop being "together" in public.[5] Some of us overfunction in some relationships and then underfunction in others, usually the less public ones. Again, evaluate your own tendencies toward underfunctioning by answering the following questions.

1. Check any characteristics of underfunctioners that describe you in some relationship, perhaps with a spouse, close friend, or family member.

    - [ ] Emotional energy focused on experiencing and expressing more than their share.
    - [ ] Entrenched in the role of the weak, dependent, vulnerable one.
    - [ ] Avoid showing competence, strength.
    - [ ] Tend to have some areas where they can't get organized.
    - [ ] Become less competent under stress, inviting others to take over.
    - [ ] Tend to develop physical or emotional symptoms under stress.
    - [ ] May be the focus of family gossip, worry, or concern.

2. In what relationship(s) do you tend to underfunction? Any ideas about why?

3. Which list of traits — overfunctioner or underfunctioner — *best* describes you? Who modeled this behavior for you (pick the most significant person)? Why is it important for you to behave this way?

THE PLACE BETWEEN

There *is* a place in between. That's what we are shooting for. Harriet Lerner says that in healthy relationships, people can move back and forth between being strong and competent (the helper) as well as being vulnerable and needy (receiving help).[6] Many of us are stuck in the overfunctioner role way too much of the time, and in too many of our relationships. I realize that your job is to help people. But I want to ask you to think seriously about what parts of yourself you use to help others. Some of the skills we've developed to be good at our jobs (independence, efficiency, task-orientation) have taken over the rest of us and we use *only* these skills all the time in all relationships. In the process, we've lost touch with our vulnerability, our need for connection, our own brokenness. We seem to have forgotten a person can't build relationships when focused on being efficient and independent. Whether you like it or not, along with all your competencies, you are also broken and wounded, needy and struggling some days. You are complicated. You are more than just a ministry machine.

If you're still unsure about the wisdom of letting people see the real you, I encourage you to take a step in that direction and see what happens. As much as I would like to promise that it will go well, I know that sometimes it doesn't. Sometimes people can't handle a leader's authenticity. But many times people are relieved, relieved that we aren't as together as we are pretending to be, and relieved that maybe they could stop faking it too.

Revealing our brokenness doesn't wipe out our strengths. We are both. Everyone is both. Take courage from Karl Wheeler, copastor of the Refuge, whom we met in chapter 5. In one of his blog entries (*www.therefugeonline.org*), he wrote the following:

> *In recovery speak, they talk about hitting our bottom. DUI, divorce, homeless[ness], bankrupt[cy], STDs all can be 'bottom' moments that begin a new direction. A few nights ago I may have hit bottom.*
>
> *I am addicted to food. Actually, I am depressed. Food is what I use to try to feel good. A quick detour for those of you who do not understand depression, or at least my version, it is the inability to experience or sometimes even imagine true pleasure. I feel numb more than anything else. Sometimes I am sad, but when I am depressed I mostly feel numb. This is where sugar comes in. You can insert in place of sugar any number of quick fixes: sex, risky behavior, beer, shopping, porn, work and success, fighting, etc. The list is much longer than this, and I have tried them all, but my favorite is always sugar. Not very glamorous, but it is my default addiction. It is a bit embarrassing in that guys are not normally talking about this addiction. The guys seem to often have work addictions, but at least they get six-figure incomes and a nice retirement. I get a huge a__ and diabetes.*
>
> *I seldom know why I am getting depressed, or even that it is happening, I just seem to not fit into any of my clothes anymore. I think sugar will make me happy. It feels good, and if it feels good, I might be happy, even if it is for the briefest of moments while I chew. This has been an especially hard season, and the darkness is fast approaching.*
>
> *Yesterday I woke with a new resolve to defeat my dependency on food, actually I always wake convinced that I will never again fall to the temptation to gorge. I drank a low-calorie nutritional drink for breakfast and had [half an] apple for lunch. Wow, I am healed.*

But the evening is what always gets me. After ten hours of sobriety, I deserve a little reward. I never have a little of anything, however. Then I always have this thought, "Oh, screw it, I am a loser and now I have blown it. I may as well go all the way." I gorged. Picture a bear at the spring salmon run, or any six-year-old left unattended in the candy store. I discovered Nutella (Nutella is a peanut butter–like concoction made of hazelnut and chocolate that Satan invented. In the periodic table it is the caloric equivalent of lead.) I began with Nutella on a graham cracker, but it felt more like a tease. Alas, there were no more crackers. The next installment was Nutella on a spoon, a large spoon. Good, but not quite enough. I needed something substantial to carry the Nutella. I found chocolate Pop-Tarts. I promise that in that moment it made perfect sense, the proper antidote to my pain. After what a civilian would have considered an excessive amount, I loaded a chocolate Pop-Tart with an inch of Nutella frosting and looked for Nirvana.

That must be a bottom. I hope it will motivate me to a new direction. I called the doctor, resolved to get back on my meds. This blog has no real point, just a confession.

P.S. Some of you might be reading, starting to feel anxious. How can we help Karl, you might wonder? Just understanding. That's all I need. And please, no favorite sugar-free Jell-O recipes.

You can see why I like Karl. He helps me feel normal and he inspires me. He's got courage and talent. And he's making a big difference in the lives of the people he ministers to, without hiding, in fact, because he's not hiding. His story is a reminder that we are all a paradox. We are all a mess some days and yet amazingly glorious on others. I understand you don't want anyone to see you on those days when you're a mess, but really, it's no big shocker. Do you really think nobody else is doing whatever it is you are doing? You may be a pastor, a ministry leader, a huge talent, someone people follow but you're just a person trying to make your way. It's okay to admit that you get lost some days. Part of being mature and healthy means getting over yourself—letting go of protecting this image of you as if it's the whole truth. Nobody, seriously, nobody has it together all the time.

Chapter 7 and 8 are focused on difficult people issues that occur in most churches and can create instability or traumatize its community. In any church there are usually some individuals whose unreasonable demands or reactions exhaust and overwhelm the leadership. Chapter 7 helps you identify these difficult personalities and offers suggestions for dealing with them. Chapter 8 specifically addresses affairs, the different types of affairs, and strategies for dealing with them.

Chapter 7

Head Shrinking

Dealing with difficult people and difficult conversations

> Consider it a sheer gift, friends, when tests and challenges come at you from all sides. You know that under pressure, your faith-life is forced into the open and shows its true colors. So don't try to get out of anything prematurely. Let it do its work so you become mature and well-developed, not deficient in any way.
>
> James 1:2 (MSG)

DIFFICULT PEOPLE

While it's true that Jesus loves us all, let's face it, some of us are harder to love than others. And if you've been working in the church for any period of time, you know what I'm talking about. Some folks just suck the life right out of you. You leave every conversation feeling like you can never do enough or get it right for them.

Difficult people (although one could surely argue that we are all difficult sometimes) come in a few varieties. Many are difficult because they've been badly hurt. Violated, abused, or abandoned in the past, they've developed aggressive, harsh, or manipulative relating styles to protect themselves from further hurt. The good news is that these individuals are simply afraid and are putting on a tough exterior to stay safe. If loved and accepted, over time they will let go of their self-protective strategies because they are no longer necessary. Other individuals, with the same characteristics, never seem to soften, no matter how much or how many people pour into their lives. The years go by and there is little or no change. They create constant drama; they continually attack, complain, and manipulate, leaving a trail of exhausted, guilt-ridden helpers behind them.

If you are dealing with someone like this, take heart—it's not you. It's possible this person has a personality disorder. People with personality disorders have difficulty functioning in *all* of their relationships—work, family, and friendships. They develop maladaptive behaviors during late adolescence or early adulthood which they continue to use pervasively—everywhere with everyone—regardless of how others respond to them. They consistently misinterpret and misperceive interactions. They say things like, "People are always out to get me," or "No one ever sees how gifted I am," or "People are always unfair to me." They can't or won't evaluate what they contribute to relational problems. They reject or defend against any negative feedback. Conflict is always the other person's fault. Their personality structures are so rigid that they don't learn from their mistakes and often have a string of broken relationships behind them.

Individuals with a personality disorder are more stuck than the average person. Most of us adjust when we get negative results. We learn that if we are demanding and controlling, people will avoid us. We learn that if we lie, people will stop trusting us. We make mistakes and then make changes. Individuals with a personality disorder don't. They just do more of the same. It's not personal. They behave this way with everyone.

It's important for you as a ministry leader to be able to identify such individuals within your church so that you can develop specific strategies for dealing with them. You'll also need to advise and protect lay leaders who are involved, or they are likely to become entangled and exhausted as well.

Identifying Personality Disorders

Therapists and other mental health workers use a diagnostic tool called the DSM-IV, which describes a series of personality disorders based on sets of symptoms. For our purposes here, I've included the diagnostic criteria for the personality disorders we most often see in our practices and churches. If you want information about any others, just google "personality disorders."

For someone to be diagnosed with a particular personality disorder, *at least* four or five of the following criteria must be present (depending on the disorder), and the characteristics must be pervasive, meaning they are found in *all* the person's relationships. If the individual has five or more of the characteristics but only behaves that way in one relationship (for example, only with the spouse or with Mom or with a church leader), then the problem is more about that particular relationship than a pervasive personality problem. Something about the relationship triggers unresolved issues, resulting in whatever negative behavior he or she exhibits. In such a case, the diagnosis *cannot* be applied.

Narcissistic (need 5 of the characteristics)

- Has a grandiose sense of self-importance
- Is preoccupied with fantasies of unlimited success, power, brilliance, beauty, or ideal love
- Believes that he or she is "special" and unique and can only be understood by other special people
- Requires excessive admiration
- Strong sense of entitlement
- Takes advantage of others to achieve his or her own ends
- Lacks empathy
- Is often envious or believes others are envious of him or her
- Arrogant affect

Borderline (need 5 of the characteristics)

- Frantic efforts to avoid real or imagined abandonment
- A pattern of unstable and intense interpersonal relationships characterized by alternating between extremes of idealization and devaluation (You're the most amazing person they have ever met one day and the most selfish, uncaring person on the planet the next.)

- Identity disturbance: markedly and persistently unstable self-image or sense of self
- Impulsivity in at least two areas that are potentially self-damaging (e.g., spending, promiscuous sex, eating disorders, substance abuse, reckless driving, binge eating)
- Recurrent suicidal behavior, gestures, threats, or self-mutilating behavior
- Affective (emotions) instability due to a marked reactivity of mood (e.g., intense depression, irritability, or anxiety usually lasting a few hours and only rarely more than a few days)
- Chronic feelings of emptiness
- Inappropriate, intense anger or difficulty controlling anger (e.g., frequent displays of temper, constant anger, recurrent physical fights)
- Transient, stress-related paranoid ideation or severe dissociative symptoms

Histrionic (need 5 of the characteristics)

- Constant seeking of reassurance or approval
- Excessive dramatics with exaggerated displays of emotions
- Excessive sensitivity to criticism or disapproval
- Inappropriately seductive appearance or behavior
- Excessive concern with physical appearance
- A need to be the center of attention (self-centeredness)
- Low tolerance for frustration or delayed gratification
- Rapidly shifting emotional states that may appear shallow to others
- Opinions are easily influenced by other people, but difficult to back up with details
- Tendency to believe that relationships are more intimate than they actually are
- Makes rash decisions
- Threatens or attempts suicide to get attention

Obsessive-Compulsive (need 4 of the characteristics)

- Preoccupation with details, rules, lists, order, organization, bodily functions, or schedules to the extent that the major point of the activity is lost
- Showing perfectionism that interferes with task completion (e.g., is unable to complete a project because his or her own overly strict standards are not met)
- Excessive devotion to work and productivity to the exclusion of leisure activities and friendships (not accounted for by obvious economic necessity)
- Being overconscientious, scrupulous, and inflexible about matters of morality, ethics, or values (not accounted for by cultural or religious identification)
- Inability to discard worn-out or worthless objects even when they have no sentimental value
- Reluctance to delegate tasks or to work with others unless they submit to exactly his or her way of doing things
- Adopting a miserly spending style toward both self and others; money is viewed as something to be hoarded for future catastrophes
- Showing rigidity and stubbornness

Paranoid (need 4 of the characteristics)

- Suspects, without sufficient basis, that others are exploiting, harming, or deceiving him or her
- Is preoccupied with unjustified doubts about the loyalty or trustworthiness of friends or associates
- Is reluctant to confide in others because of unwarranted fear that the information will be used maliciously against him or her
- Reads hidden demeaning or threatening meanings in benign remarks or events
- Persistently bears grudges (i.e., is unforgiving of insults, injuries, or slights)

- Perceives attacks on his or her character or reputation that are not apparent to others and is quick to react angrily or to counterattack
- Has recurrent suspicions, without justification, regarding fidelity of spouse or sexual partner

A word of caution: This is just enough information to make you dangerous. Once you've looked at the criteria, you may find yourself thinking, "Oh, that totally describes Frank. I wonder if I should tell him what I've discovered." The answer is an emphatic *no*. Remember, these individuals are reactive. Rather than responding with delight over your insightful observation, they will likely retaliate in some way. It works about as well as telling someone they're fat. You can see the problem clearly, but pointing it out is just going to be painful and make them mad.

Responding to Persons with Personality Disorders

Boundaries, boundaries, boundaries! You are in ministry because you are caring, and the fact that you want to make a difference is a very good thing. But you won't always be able to help everyone. It's important to give yourself permission to "fail" this person. What I mean by "fail" is to not meet their expectations or even your own. It is unlikely that the person will experience much, if any, growth, and it is very likely that they will be disappointed in you. So you need to define the standard of care in these cases not by the extensive needs of this person but by what is realistic for you or others to give without sacrificing other relationships and responsibilities.

Focusing on boundaries is not just for your protection. It is also the most loving thing to do for them. Individuals with personality disorders tend to gravitate to people who have no boundaries, who will abandon their own needs and relationships to rescue them. But this only reinforces their patterns. It's in their best interest to have to live with the tension of people saying no to them, to have to wait, to have to handle things on their own. They are not likely to agree that this is good for them, but it does offer the opportunity for a baby step of growth.

Get specific about what your boundaries will be. Will you take calls late at night? Will you go to the police station to bail them out again? Will you go to the hospital after they have had another accident, another fight, another sexual violation? Will you lend them more money?

Think through the following questions and answer them based on what is truly realistic for you. If you are dealing with more than one person with a personality disorder, consider appropriate responses for each individual.

1. How many times a week/month will I talk with this person?
2. How much time will I spend in those conversations?
3. What things will we focus on during those conversations?
4. What requests/conversations must I consistently say no to?

This is hard work, so it's important not to go it alone. Talk with others about how you will handle a particular situation. Agree together on a strategy so you feel prepared and supported.

Communicate very directly to persons with a personality disorder about what's appropriate, or about what you and your community are willing to give. You may have to be more direct than you might naturally be. For example, "I won't be able to talk to you more than once a week so I need you to limit your calls in between."

Be careful about the kinds of activities in which you involve these people. They generally do not do well in a small-group setting because they tend to overpower the group, taking it hostage with their crises, demands, and reactivity. It's important to protect group members from such individuals, finding a way to ease them out of the group into a one-on-one situation or professional care. They may react in hurt or anger, but remind yourself that each person in the group is important and that the whole must not be sacrificed to meet the demands of one.

I asked Georgia, a member of the pastoral team of a large church, to tell me what she's learned about helping difficult people:

How do you know when you're dealing with a difficult person?

"People who are in pain look the same initially. Their needs are the same. And you need to come alongside. Then we look for some progress. Someone may still have a long way to go but when there's movement, we stay with her. Others, you can see over time, this isn't going to go well, it's a no-win.

"For example, we have someone who I think might be borderline. She sends me these bizarre, manipulative emails about how the church isn't loving her or helping her even though I know there are people involved with her, trying to help. She says they're not doing it right and should be reprimanded. I look at it this way, there are two kinds of people—the apple people—the people you can be journeying with and see growth happen, and the orange people—who don't really want to change. With the oranges, beware! I've watched people put apple maneuvers on the orange—it's just not going to work. In this case, the two people who were trying to help were more codependent, with no boundaries, so I actually told them to disengage. For their own health it was necessary for them to get out. So then I hear from the orange again, that these people have an obligation to be there and love her. I told her that this was not biblical, that people have the right to choose to be her friend or not. She didn't like this and wants to go bigger, write letters, confront them. I'm planning to talk to her again, I want to say, 'It's been three years. Can I share with you what I'm seeing?'

"We've developed a strategy as a staff. We identify these people and assign them a staff member. They tend to go from one staff member to another because nobody is good enough. We talk about it in our meetings. 'Prepare yourself, so-and-so is upset and is probably going to call you. Just refer them back to me' (or whoever is designated as their contact person). This has really worked for us. It keeps us from all getting sucked into the same problem with the same person.

"It's hard to relate to people in this way. I'm bent toward listening. I want to walk it through with people for a while, but it is important to pay attention to your spirit and your gut. To recognize the internal stuff. When I talk to this person I'm anxious, I feel bad, a little scared. Something about this person doesn't feel safe at all. Sometimes I just feel slimed. That's a sign. They do such a good job of playing with your mind. They make you feel like crap. You start doubting yourself. I have to talk myself through it and remind myself that I really love people no matter what they say. Don't get sucked in, it's like a vortex, it just gets worse and worse. Then they have you and it's so horrible!"

So what do you do?
"Don't give your home phone (if you can avoid it). Don't give them a lot of time. Even though the emails sound very urgent or threatening, I take my time and think through what I'm going to do. They are not in control of my life. Respond like you would to other people. Don't rearrange your priority list for them. You can *care* but you can't *carry* people. And it's important to network with therapists. That's such a help, so I can bounce things off. I can explain what's going on and ask if I'm just weird or what."

Pay Attention to Your Gut Reaction

One of the biggest struggles for people who really care about helping is trying to live with the tension of a difficult person's needs against everyone else's. When you start to second-guess yourself, ask yourself: Is it true that I am unloving and judgmental (or whatever you are being accused of)? Do I consistently protect myself from others; am I cold or anxious or fearful in my other relationships? Maybe you *are* struggling right now and many of your relationships *are* difficult. If that's the case, there's something going on inside you that needs attention. But if it's true that you generally move toward people in need, that you generally get involved, and that you genuinely care, there's likely something about this particular person that is creating a negative response in you. Georgia's advice is right on the money. Pay attention to your internal reactions. If it feels icky, if you just know it's going to get ugly, you may be intuitively picking up on a person's personality disorder before you see all the evidence of it.

HAVING DIFFICULT CONVERSATIONS

Sometimes it's not so much that a person is difficult, but rather that we have to have a difficult conversation. Nobody (well almost nobody) likes conflict, but it's a normal, natural part of relationships. It's also normal to feel anxious and make mistakes in attempting to handle it. But dealing with problems doesn't have to be big and dramatic. With planning and practice we can learn to work through difficulties in ways that deepen our relationships rather than destroy them.

The key is preparation. Whether it's a conversation with a family member or coworker or friend, thinking through what you want to accomplish beforehand will increase your chances of having a successful interaction. If you go into the conversation without planning ahead, you are more likely to get yourself in trouble.

Think through your goals. What is the problem as you see it? What are you hoping to accomplish with this conversation? Be honest with yourself. Sometimes our goals are unrealistic or unproductive and we'll only intensify the conflict if we pursue them. Here are some unproductive or unrealistic goals to avoid:

- *Trying to change the other person*—They're doing something you don't want them to do and you hope that this conversation will make them stop.
- *Trying to make them agree with you*—You think their perspective is wrong and you hope that explaining your perspective will cause them to give up theirs.
- *Trying to solve a difficult or long-term problem in one conversation*—You are tired of this problem and are anxious to get it taken care of once and for all.
- *Trying to get an apology*—The other person has hurt you and you want to confront them so they will feel bad and say they are sorry.
- *Venting your feelings so you will feel better*—Your feelings are overwhelming and your focus is getting them off your chest.

While it's okay to feel any of these things, we need to be realistic about what can actually be accomplished. In any conflict, we're dealing with another person with their own perspective and their own needs. Our approach needs to address that.

Preparing for the Conversation

Think through what you want to say. Write it down. Ask yourself how the other person might react; consider how you might react if someone said this to you. Focus on communicating your feelings and your hopes and don't dwell on their behavior, which might feel like an attack. Make sure that what you say invites dialogue. Acknowledge that this is only your perspective and you realize they may see things differently. Ask them to explain their perspective to you. Use a phrase such as, "Help me understand ...," to do this.

Here are some examples of how you might begin the conversation:

- "The other day in staff meeting, I felt embarrassed after the comment you made about my idea. Can you help me understand what you meant by that?"
- "You and I seem to be on edge with each other all the time lately. Maybe we could talk about that. I'm wondering what's bothering you."

If things get heated, often it's a good idea to stop the conversation before too many things are said that could intensify the conflict. "I'm having trouble figuring out what to say next. I think I need to take a break and finish this later."

You might want to express yourself using what I call the "sandwich approach." You put the white fluffy bread — what you appreciate about the other person, how you value the relationship, that you want things to be better — at the beginning and end of the conversation.

The meat—your concern, what you're upset about—goes in the middle. This helps the other person better receive what you are saying and reminds both of you that the relationship is worth working for.

If You Are on the Receiving End of a Difficult Conversation

What if you're the recipient of difficult words from another person? Here are some things to bear in mind to help you through it:

1. Focus on understanding the concern of the other person rather than defending yourself. Though it feels awkward, taking notes can help you focus on listening.
2. Ask exploring questions, without expressing an opinion or attitude. "What do you mean by …? How were you feeling when I said …? So you thought I meant …?" Listening validates the other person's feelings and helps calm the conversation, but remember: validating is not the same as agreeing or accepting blame. It's just acknowledging that you hear and respect their perspective.
3. Restate what you've heard. "So what you're upset about is. … "
4. Ask what change they would like to see. This doesn't mean you will do what they're asking, it's just about clarifying for both of you what they are looking for. They may say they aren't asking for any change, they just wanted to be heard.
5. If something needs to be done, ask for time to think about what you've heard. Then come back to it later when you know what you want to do with it.

YOUR TURN

1. How do you generally respond to conflict? Do you confront, ignore, avoid, feel overwhelmed, get controlling? If you're not sure, ask other people in your life. They can tell you.

2. Think of a specific person or conflict you currently need to deal with. What's the problem as you see it?

3. What are your goals in this specific situation? Based on what you learned in this chapter, are any of them unproductive or unrealistic?

(cont.)

4. How could you express those goals briefly and gently, without attacking or blaming?

5. How do you think the other person might respond?

6. What next step could you take to begin dealing with this conflict?

For more help in with dealing with difficult people, the book *Safe People* by Henry Cloud and John Townsend (Zondervan, 1996) is an excellent resource.

Chapter 8

We've Got Issues

Handling affairs and sexual addictions

> Brothers and sisters, if someone is caught in a sin, you who live by the Spirit should restore that person gently. But watch yourselves, or you also may be tempted. Carry each other's burdens, and in this way you will fulfill the law of Christ.
>
> Galatians 6:1–2

Sadly, affairs and sexual addictions are happening in ever increasing numbers in our churches. Chances are, if you haven't already dealt with them, you will soon. When they happen, they often rock the whole church, which can be overwhelming for those who have to clean up the mess. When people problems get this big, it's hard to continue to pursue authenticity, but it's vital that you do. Churches and families can survive and even thrive in spite of this kind of trauma ... *if* they can lean into the pain; have the hard, honest conversations necessary; and develop a plan about how they will walk through restoration together.

Here's what I often see in my office. A Christian couple comes in shaken and terrified because the husband's affair (although the numbers of cheating wives is growing) or pornography use has just been discovered. The wife is devastated. The husband is humiliated and often desperate to hold on to his family. Their family, friends, and faith community are shocked and unsure of what to do: Do they advise divorce, or urge them to work it out? Do they get involved or send them outside the church for help? Should the offending spouse be asked to leave the church or embraced as a wounded person needing healing? These are complex questions with no black-and-white answers.

If you've never struggled with sexual sin (or if you do but are pretending you don't), it's hard to want to help someone who so blatantly sins against their spouse and children. But recognize that as messy as sexual sin is, the behavior is a symptom of something else. Bad behavior is usually motivated by pain. People don't just wake up one day and decide to cheat on their spouse and destroy their families. They've already been struggling for a long time. Whether the pain comes from unresolved issues from their history or their current disconnection from others, they are lost and floundering. And so they cross a line they never thought they would. That doesn't excuse them from responsibility for their choices, but it does help you maintain perspective that people are more than their bad choices.

Sometimes people won't want to deal with their sexual sins and then there's little you can do but send them on their way before they create more damage. Others have been longing for years for someone to see the mess they are in and point them in the direction of healing. These folks often respond humbly and eagerly to help.

Walking people through recovery is lengthy and emotional. I recommend creating a team of caregivers, some of whom have previously dealt with either addictions or affairs, to partner with you. And immediately involve a therapist you trust to work closely with the family and to advise your team. I suggest a therapist because often the issues surrounding sexual sin are layered and confusing. Someone with expertise in the dynamics of sexual sin will be able to help the couple explore not only the pain of the affair but also its roots and the issues in the marriage that will need to be addressed in order for the couple to move forward.

Beyond those initial steps, the first thing to do is to determine the kind of affair you are dealing with. This will dictate the kind of help that will be most useful.

KINDS OF AFFAIRS

When I work with couples dealing with an affair, I try to put myself inside the offending spouse's head and ask, "What kind of statement does the affair make?" Here are the four statements I see most often.

1. "I can do whatever I want."

In this case, the person who cheated on his or her spouse:

- shows no shame or remorse over the affair;
- lacks concern regarding the impact of their actions on the family;
- believes their own needs must be met regardless of the feelings of others;
- often views their spouse as a possession to keep or toss (they may also be physically or emotionally abusive);
- uses power to manipulate people in other areas of their life;
- believes their money, power, position, or talent makes them special, entitled.

Fortunately, this type of affair comprises the smallest group we as leaders will have to deal with. Offenders are generally not interested in church, unless they can be in charge of, say, their own cult! Unfortunately, they are the hardest to help. Conversation after conversation yields the same results. You confront in love but see no remorse or sadness, only anger and defensiveness. The offending party may even deny the affair happened, regardless of clear evidence. Because they are not open to help (perhaps because of a personality disorder; see chapter 7), your attention must shift to supporting the spouse and children to minimize further damage. As for the offender, negative consequences are your only option. They need to be told that their affair and lack of integrity in facing it cannot be tolerated or ignored since such behavior poses a threat to the well-being of their family and the community as a whole. Paul warns the church, "I am writing to you that you must not associate with any who claim to be fellow believers but are sexually immoral" (1 Cor. 5:11).

2. "I want out of this marriage."

In this case, the person who cheated on his or her spouse:

- is very dissatisfied with the marriage;
- may have tried to create change in the past but is fed up, no longer making an effort;
- is emotionally distant from the spouse and family, very "checked out";
- is focused on taking care of their own needs;
- rather than deal with things directly, chooses to sabotage the marriage with an affair to create a crisis and force an end.

This relationship is difficult to save because the spouse who cheated is generally more invested in the affair than the marriage. They may say that they are in love with this other person and anxious to get on with their new life together. As such, the spouse and children may be seen as barriers rather than broken hearts to deal with. Again, if the offender's continual response is anger and defensiveness or a list of what's wrong with the spouse, it's likely that they are not interested in any kind of restoration. Your job here will be to help the injured spouse adjust to the reality of their situation, perhaps by pointing them toward legal and/or financial assistance. The family will need plenty of support and possibly protection from further injury if the cheater carelessly moves ahead with their own agenda. The offender may also need to be asked to leave your fellowship.

3. "Look what you made me do!"

In this case, the person who cheated on his or her spouse:

- is very angry, hurt, and hopeless;
- doesn't know how to successfully communicate dissatisfaction;

- is confused or ambivalent about the marriage;
- uses the affair to take care of unmet needs in the marriage;
- may feel emotional attachment to the other person, yet still express love for their spouse;
- uses the affair to communicate their unhappiness, or as a wake-up call to the spouse—to force some kind of change.

In this instance there is more hope for the marriage. The individual's behavior is much more about getting the spouse's attention than it is about getting out of the marriage. The affair may have been done in a very "in your face" kind of way, guaranteeing exposure. This couple can recover over time if both parties are willing to work hard at changing the patterns in the marriage that led to their disconnect from one another, and assuming that the offending party is truly remorseful. While the Bible certainly provides permission to end any marriage where adultery has occurred, encourage the couple to give it some time and be open to what God might be calling them to in their particular situation—and remind them that many couples have recovered and improved their relationship after these kinds of affairs. Also urge them to see a good therapist as soon as possible to help them evaluate their options. A small group of experienced, caring people can make a huge impact as they provide a safe place for each spouse to express what's going on during the recovery process.

4. "I'm out of control. Help me!"

In this case, the person who cheated on his or her spouse:

- is likely a sex addict who often began with a compulsive use of porn which has escalated into a relationship or encounter(s) with real people;
- sees the affair as purely physical (little or no emotional attachment to the person; the other person is otherwise irrelevant);
- uses sex as a stress reliever, medicator, a "high";
- is very secretive, going to great lengths to hide the affair or porn use;

- expresses great shame and disgust over their behavior which they feel unable to control;
- may desperately want to stay married, may deeply love their spouse and children;
- may express relief when the affair is revealed.

This situation is very different than the others and it's what I see most often in my office—Christian men and women who love their families and are active in their churches but who are addicted to sex. They show up at their kids' soccer games and PTA meetings, but have lunch at a strip club or have sex with a coworker when away on business. These individuals are often deeply disturbed by their behavior and desperately want out, but have no idea what to do with themselves. When caught, they are often extremely remorseful and in a panic to hold on to their families.

Helping this type of family involves educating yourself about sexual addiction. If dealing with this topic is new to you, I would suggest reading *Contrary to Love* (Hazelden, 1994) by Patrick Carnes, an expert in this area, or *False Intimacy* (NavPress, 1997) by Dr. Harry Schaumburg. It may be difficult for you (especially if you are female) to manage your own reactions to sexually addictive behaviors. It's hard to understand how the man who looks like a great dad and serves on your church elder board can be the same man who goes to massage parlors or picks up prostitutes. It can be hard not to express your disgust either directly or subtly. But addicts already feel disgusted with themselves. That's why they have been living a secret life. They know they are out of control and living in sin.

It's certainly useful and appropriate for those who have a close relationship with this person to express their pain, anger, and disappointment about the person's double life. But if the sharing becomes focused on shaming, this person will likely only go further underground. What addicts need is an invitation to deal with their addiction; help looks like the opportunity for regular accountability and support. They will need a good therapist to explore the reasons they are using sex to self-soothe, possibly a sex addicts group (Alcoholics Anonymous sponsors them in many cities), as well as a small group in their church where they can experience authentic community as they pursue healing.

UNDERSTANDING THE SEX ADDICT

In the first stage of recovery, the addict's focus will be to abstain from unhealthy sexual behaviors. Without sex to medicate, the issues underlying the behavior will surface. In order to successfully overcome the addiction long-term, the addict will need to address the internal struggle that propels them toward self-destructive behavior. According to Patrick Carnes, the sex addict struggles with five negative core beliefs:

1. I am basically a bad, unworthy person.
2. No one would love me as I am.
3. My needs are never going to be met if I have to depend on others.
4. Sex is my most important need.
5. I am bad because sex is my most important need.

These beliefs developed out of a painful childhood. Typically, this person has been emotionally and/or physically abused. They have often been sexually abused or exposed to sexually explicit material or behaviors at an early age. (For example, an eight-year-old boy finds his dad's or neighbor's *Playboy* magazines and experiences pleasure or escape from his reality as he looks at the pictures.) Often there are other addicts in their family of origin. As adults, addicts have great difficulty with emotional intimacy and may struggle with additional addictions or compulsions. Over time, they need more intense "highs" to achieve the same sense of relief. Each experience reinforces the behavior which becomes more and more compulsive, and sometimes more deviant.[7]

While it's important for those helping the addict to have compassion, in my opinion every addict, regardless of the addiction—sex, food, alcohol, drugs, gambling—has a choice. Whatever our histories—abuse, molestation, abandonment—we are still responsible for the choices we make as adults. I have seen people with the most horrendous stories choose to be loving parents and partners. Yes, our histories can make it hard for us to make healthy choices, but I believe freedom is possible for everyone. We will have to fight for it, but God's power in us is big enough to conquer anything.

GENERAL STRATEGIES FOR DEALING WITH AFFAIRS

In my opinion, the use of pornography is cheating. Whether or not another person is physically present, the porn user fantasizes (and typically masturbates) about having sex with someone else. This is adultery and Jesus clearly defines it as such in Matthew 5:28. That's why women feel so violated by their husband's porn use. So avoid the temptation to minimize the spouse's pain by suggesting it's less damaging than an affair in person.

1. Validate the spouse's pain.

Shock, anger, disgust, devastation, and betrayal are all normal responses to an affair. Expect a range of intense, roller-coaster emotions for a long time. You can help by acknowledging the spouse's feelings and allowing them to be where they are. Each person will need to work through their emotions at their own pace. As their listening ear, you will get over the affair far more quickly than they will and you may be tempted to try to hurry them along. It often takes years to recover and the first year is particularly brutal.

Nobody deserves this. There are some things that people should never do to each other and this is one of them. Even if the spouse has been a lousy partner, there are other choices the adulterer could have made. Allow even a bad spouse to express their hurt. Over time each partner will need to face how they contributed to the state of their marriage, but initially the pain of betrayal will overwhelm everything.

2. Leave decisions about reconciliation or divorce to the couple.

As noted earlier, while it's important to affirm the biblical permission to end the marriage (especially for types 1 and 2, see pages 119 – 120), encourage the couple to take time to evaluate what God might be calling them to in their particular situation. This is not, I repeat, *not* your decision to make. Your job is to answer questions on theological issues regarding sexual sin and to provide support for each party as they decide what to do with their lives. No doubt some couples will ask you to tell them what to do, and it's tempting, especially when the answer seems clear to you. But this is not your life and you will not live with the consequences of the decision. So unless it is a case of abuse, hands off!

HELPING KIDS THROUGH AN AFFAIR

What if a kid finds out about a parent's affair before their mom or dad knows, and confides in you about it? This is a secret that's too big for a child or teen to carry. Treat it like you would information about someone who is suicidal. Tell the child that this is an adult problem, you're glad they told you about it, and you will take responsibility for getting their family some help. Then get some trusted adults involved. Go to the person who is having the affair and let them know you are aware of the situation and want to help. Do not reveal that the information came from their child, just that you've learned about it and are very concerned for their family. It's important to protect the child from being punished or feeling responsible for whatever might happen to the family as a result of the revelation.

Once a parent's affair has been made public, provide opportunities for the child to vent as often as they need to. Make sure they have access to someone who can be available to them if it can't be you. Let them know they can feel anything they want to about this situation, that their anger, disgust, fear, confusion, whatever, make sense and are natural reactions. Remind them that this is a problem between their parents and they are in no way responsible for causing it or fixing it. Help them focus on their own lives. Their parents are likely too distracted with their own chaos to really be in touch with what's going on with their kids. This child will need someone to fill in the gap until things stabilize at home.

HOW DO WE KNOW IF PEOPLE ARE TRULY PURSUING RESTORATION?

Whatever people are dealing with, the path to emotional health and spiritual growth looks the same. It starts with *confession*, an honest and open conversation about what's going on.

I'm not a big fan of public, all-church confessions. I think it's far more useful to involve a small group of people who are already involved in the life of this person. In such an environment, a thorough confession can be a cleansing experience for the adulterer. Hopefully, this group will be part of a restoration team that will walk through the process with the family. In terms of notifying the church as a whole, this can be done in a more general way, initially by someone in leadership (if the family is well known or the church is very small) and possibly down the road by the adulterer, once they have actually made some progress on their recovery and understand both the pain they have caused and the issues that led to their behavior.

How people talk about their struggles and sin has a lot to do with whether they will experience freedom and restoration. Someone who is continually defensive about their behavior or focused on how it was someone else's fault is still stuck. They are not likely to make much progress. Remind them that while bad things may have happened to them and their spouse may have failed them, the only way out of this mess is to look it square in the face and deal with their part in it.

Someone who is really ready for change understands this intuitively. They are already open to self-discovery and willing to take responsibility for the pain they have caused. I see this most often in men who are struggling with sexual addictions and have felt trapped by their compulsive behaviors. These men may have begun leaving clues or dropping hints in the hopes of being found out because they are desperate for help. They will talk openly about what has happened without trying to protect themselves from looking bad. They will tolerate their partner's anger and despair even though it's very difficult.

While it's not necessary to hear all the gory details of each time they fell, people do need to share the depth and breadth of their sin in order to feel that they've actually confessed. For example, these are some questions you might want to address:

- How long has this behavior been going on? When and how did it start?
- How many people were they involved with?
- What happened, generally? (Some will argue that anything less than penetration does not count as adultery. This denial needs to be confronted.)
- Have their children ever seen any of these events?
- How much money have they spent on this behavior?
- Did they ever force someone to have sex or perform a sex act?
- Were there ever minors involved? (If so, you'll be required to report this information to police and/or child protective services. Crimes against minors are not protected by confidentiality.)
- Have they been tested for STDs? (This has often never crossed their mind. They should be encouraged to do this immediately, as should their spouse.)

Caution: The offended spouse needs to decide how much of this information they want to know. They may or may not want to be a part of this particular conversation. Some will ask detailed questions only to be tormented by the information later. Help them think through what information they need in order to understand the extent of what happened and what questions should perhaps remain unasked for their own healing. Ultimately, this is their decision, not the offending spouse's or a third party's.

This conversation is hard for everyone but needs to happen. Otherwise the offending partner may feel as if they are getting away with something, or that they're accepted only because nobody knows how badly they behaved. When people tell you the basic details, try not to flinch. If you're shocked, don't show it. If you want to throw up, take a deep breath. If you're disgusted, remind yourself you've done disgusting things too. People will stop talking if it appears to them that you can't handle it. Just nod your head as if you hear this stuff all day long.

Eventually, if you're serious about authenticity, this will be true and it won't seem so overwhelming. Being a safe place for people means learning to tolerate hearing things that sometimes you'd just rather not.

After confession, we want to *help people explore why they do the things they do*. You don't have to be a therapist to do this. And don't feel like you have to walk through the whole process with them, but you can get them started with some very basic questions, such as:

- When and how were you first exposed to sexual sin?
- Is there someone in your life you learned this behavior from? Were there affairs going on in your family of origin?
- What need do you think sexual sin met in your life?

Just these few questions will give people a good start toward exploring their patterns.

Once individuals have explored their behavior, and this can take weeks to do, they'll eventually be *ready to make a plan for change*. True repentance has this element to it. Some people will be content to just talk about what's happened in the past and how they've struggled forever. Remorse and regret are important but are not enough to create change. Those who are really repentant want to move on. They want to know how they can be different. That's how you'll know if you're investing in someone who's truly interested in growth.

When you're trying to help someone develop a plan for change, don't take responsibility for all the ideas. Ask them to read books on the subject or encourage them to talk to someone in your community who has had success dealing with affairs. Then break the plan down into doable baby steps. Take into consideration the other stressors (time/money limitations) in their life. Let people be in charge of deciding what is reasonable for them, then be their cheerleader.

Remember, all this is going to take longer than you want it to. Sometimes a lot longer. But you don't have to do it all. Use small groups, mentors, therapists, support groups, whatever's available to help with someone in crisis.

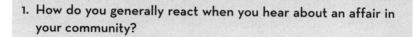
YOUR TURN

1. How do you generally react when you hear about an affair in your community?

2. What's been your personal experience with affairs or sex addiction, and how might that experience impact your reaction?

Chapter 9

Analyze That

What authenticity looks like on the journey

> I want you woven into a tapestry of love, in touch with everything there is to know of God. Then you will have minds confident and at rest, focused on Christ, God's great mystery.
>
> Colossians 2:2 (MSG)

Hannah was raised by wolves. With a pedophile for a dad and an abusive, paranoid mom, she didn't have much of a chance. And yet when you meet her, what you experience is this smart, funny woman. She shouldn't be this amazing and yet she is. Of course, she has some deep wounds. She is afraid to enjoy being a woman because she's been violated. She finds it hard to open up to people because her mom taught her that no one can be trusted. She's ashamed of her history because, in her family, horrible secrets must be taken to the grave. She's in a lot of pain but she can fake it with the best of them.

Hannah spent most of her life in one church or another, but in recent years has quit attending. She loves Jesus but the church has not been a safe place for her. After working together to heal some of the pain of her abuse, we began to talk about her present loneliness and her need for relationships with other women, and I suggested that she consider looking for a new church and small group. She decided to give it a try and got involved in a women's Bible study.

At first, the experience went well. The pastor's wife and the group leader took a special interest in Hannah and made her feel welcome. But as weeks went by, things began to go south. Hannah was ready to be real—to tell the truth about herself and her frustrations with following Jesus in the middle of the mess of her life—but the more open she was, the more distant the other women became. She came in one day and told me, "The group leader talks to us like children. This week she wrote the definition for *obedience* on the board. She told us obedience means 'to obey immediately, completely, and cheerfully.' It was all I could do not to laugh. Does she really believe that? And who does that?" Hannah's in trouble because in this particular church, it's against the rules to say that you're not okay and don't know when you will be. All I can do is say I'm sorry.

Hannah's experience with her small group is not unusual. All too often, well-intentioned people gather together to try to create growth but instead slow it down or grind it to a halt. How do we know if what we're offering fosters transformation or just gives people something to do? We can't go by numbers of people involved or by dollars in the offering plate. Those things tell us something but not enough. The best measurement is to talk with the people involved. Not just the leaders but the participants themselves. Ask them what they are learning, what they are working on, how this activity or group is challenging or encouraging them. The question is always, "Are we growing, and in what ways?"

While the road to authenticity and emotional health is long and winding, it will eventually become obvious when we are making progress. We will know because we will see it happening. People will be doing more than understanding or articulating biblical concepts, they'll actually be living out these truths. They will understand them experientially as well as intellectually. They'll say, "I get what forgiveness really looks like now," "I know what repentance requires," "I'm able to love in ways I never could before." They will experience a greater sense of excitement, freedom, and joy.

GROWING AS A GROUP

About four years ago I was approached by a group of women in their twenties and thirties who wanted some help starting a process group. They were a large group, twelve or so at the time, most of whom had known each other since junior high but felt their relationships were lacking depth. I worked with them for a year and they have continued to meet ever since. Their group experience is changing their lives because they have committed themselves to authenticity and to supporting one another's growth. I visited them recently and asked them to tell you about their group.

Why do you guys still do this group?

"It's a constant community. No matter what's going on in my life, if my job changes or whatever, I've got a group of people who are consistent and know everything about me" (Stacey)

"These are the people in my life who really know me; I don't have to pretend here. There's no masks or facades. It's a chance in the week to be absolutely real." (Stephanie)

"It's a safe haven; if I just have to unload something, I can feel very safe in doing that. Maybe no one else in my life will understand but they will. They get me." (Emily)

"It's exhausting to manage our image — our work, [our] mommy image. It's good to have a place where you don't have to do that. You can just say what's going on and I'm sorry if that's ugly. This kind of sharing allows us to truly bear each others' burdens." (Amy)

How has this process changed you?

"By telling my story, not only did I have to get real with other people, I had to get real with myself — to focus on the things in my life that needed improving. I've experienced a lot of growth in my life. I'm not the same person I was when I started the group. If I'm struggling with something or feeling blue, my husband will say, 'Just wait till Wednesday,' because he knows this is the place where I can come and dump it out and because they all know me so well, they know how that relates to everything else. I have this large group of women who I can call any time and say, 'I had a really bad morning,' and every single one of them will know what that means for me. You can't find that anywhere else." (Stephanie)

"If I didn't have this group, I don't know where I'd be right now. I didn't know that what I was living in [domestic violence] was not appropriate or not okay. I really thought, 'This is my life. I chose this and this is how it is.' I just put this face out to the world like everything's okay. I had been living like that and nobody knew. Once I started having these relationships and talking about it, my life changed. I had best friends but they had no idea. I just wouldn't tell them that. I didn't know how to. If I hadn't gone through this whole deepening process, well, it's kind of scary to me. It just all happened at the right time and it's been truly life changing for me. I feel like my old life is behind me and I have many more years of this new one, that's amazing, with my husband. I'm just so glad I'm not there anymore." (Emily)

"The cool thing is that all the work Emily and her husband went through to make their marriage better has made my marriage better. I've learned from her. It all feeds back in." (Stephanie)

"This group has allowed me to be closer to my non-Christian friends because I'm letting go of the image of the kind of Christian I thought I was supposed to be. Now I can finally be real and love them the way I want to. This feels like a new kind of Christianity." (Amy)

"It's important for us to do this for other people now. To really ask how they are, really see them. I know I can't have intimate relationships with everyone but I can at least do this. Isn't this what we should be modeling to nonbelievers—sharing the struggles, really asking and caring?" (Emily)

"But that life-changing thing takes a long time. In the beginning it's scary and awkward and you feel sort of forced into an intimacy that's not really there yet but you get to it. We had to be taught to put our images away, to leave them in the car before you come in." (Amy)

Kelly, you're new to the group. What's this experience been like for you so far?

"I've never done anything remotely like this in my life and when I was first invited to join, there was a lot of consternation there for me. Not because of the specific people here but because of me. It's been a total journey. Walking in tonight, everyone was praying for Amy and all she had to say was, 'It's my dad,' and I knew what that meant because I know Amy's story. To be able to share on that level is awesome. I have long-standing friends that I've had for years but never shared with like this. This is new for me. I feel really lucky to be in this group. This is enriching my life, making me a better wife, mother, person."

I know you're scared about telling your story. What are you afraid might happen?

"I'll take the step to do it even though it's horribly uncomfortable. It's pretty much horrendous to me. I have kids. I'm afraid that after I tell my story, people might think, 'Maybe Kelly wouldn't be the person I would swap babysitting with.' It's the first time I've really cared what people thought of me. It's a different kind of investment. And everyone here is quite aware of how difficult this is for me."

What are some of the problems for you as a group?

"People outside the group recognize there's something going on here and that it's real. That's hard. Our group is seen as elitist and closed but you can't do this unless the group is closed. It's hard for people who don't have something like this to understand why you can't have a revolving door." (Stephanie)

How do you deal with conflict in the group?

"We learned a lot from our first big conflict. Some group members had discussed a problem within the group and came up with their own solution but when they presented it, it came across badly." (CholeAnne)

"We all talked for days after that to try [to] diffuse the hurt." (Amy)

"After that big blow-up, our relationships have been so much closer. I don't think other conflicts will get that big again, because our relationships are different now." (CholeAnne)

"I feel more confident about confronting conflict. It's still not comfortable and a tough thing to do but now that we've been through that experience and everybody has still chosen to be here, I think there's a lot of power in that. Emily and I might have had an argument but she's still choosing to sit beside me on the couch and be invested in my life, and that has power in it." (Stephanie)

"We've learned that if you've got a problem with somebody, address it before it gets too big so you can resolve it in a peaceful way." (Emily)

"As a newcomer who was skeptical about talking about things that bother us about each other, I was amazed by the effective communication that goes on in the group, and how committed the group is to accomplishing its goals." (Kelly)

What happens when the group loses its way?

"There was a time when the group wasn't staying on task. We were just chatting. It didn't feel worth the time to go, and I was mourning the loss of the intimacy level. But we talked about that and then put some structure in place to get back to our goals. Intimacy doesn't happen through chitchat." (Emily)

"We all acknowledge that we talk to each other outside of group but when you bring up something negative, don't say, 'Emily and I were talking....' Just bring it forward as your own concern." (Stephanie)

What do you want to say to other people about this experience?

"Holding it all in is exhausting, I don't think people know that because that's all they know how to do. I'm always wanting to start up a group for people. I want to say, 'You need this too, you'll feel so much freer.'" (Emily)

"It's so incredible how intertwined our lives have become. This Monday I was having a low day and nobody knew that because I didn't want to talk about it, but Emily and Stacey, who had no clue about what was going on, both left messages on my answering machine that day that totally helped that situation." (CholeAnne)

"I think this kind of group sort of reverses what the church may have ingrained into us. It's so important to have this and multiply this." (Amy)

Transformation is exciting! These women are experiencing something with each other that is revolutionizing their lives. That's what we're looking for. Be seeker-sensitive if you want, be postmodern if you want, use cutting-edge technology if you want ... but above all, teach your people how to love and how to change their lives. Without that, the rest is clanging cymbals.

HELP FOR EVALUATING CHANGE

One of the things therapists do as we work with clients is to stop along the way and ask ourselves whether the individual, couple, or family is functioning better. We want to know if our strategies are effective or if we need to do something differently. We consider what change has or hasn't occurred. Are their relationships improving, are their fears and anxiety lessening, are they making healthier choices, managing stress better? Are they more connected to God, more honest about their struggles with him, more confident in his love or his forgiveness?

The church can ask these same questions when evaluating its impact. Ask yourself if you are observing these things:

- Are people discovering new things about themselves?
- Can they articulate areas of growth they are working on?
- Are they asking questions/expressing doubts?
- Are they connecting with each other in- and outside of church events?
- Do they have a strong sense of belonging to at least a few others in the body of Christ?
- Are they sharing pain/failure/struggle even while in the midst of it?
- Can they accept each others' different perspectives?
- Can they be honest about how they experience each other; can they talk about what they need from each other?

- Are they addressing conflict among themselves?
- Is our leadership (am I) participating, sharing personally with others?

Spend time with people individually or ask to attend their small group meetings and invite them to talk about how the church is or isn't nurturing their emotional health and spiritual growth. At first this might feel terrifying and invasive but as we build a culture that values growth and authenticity, such dialogue will become normal and natural. It's not about checking up on each other, it's about having real conversations about what's actually happening in each others' lives. When we know what people are really dealing with, we can better develop structures that address and support those issues.

The most telling place to evaluate our growth is at home. Are we better at loving our families? It's easier to bring a homeless person a lunch once a week than it is to stop being sarcastic with your husband when you're irritated. The people that live with us can tell us if we are making any progress. Is our home a safer, kinder place for the people we are most responsible for? Encourage people to occasionally ask their family members, "Have you seen any growth or change in me in the last year? What areas do you think I need to work on that I might not be aware of?"

The more often people talk about or hear others talk about intentional change, the more normative it will become in your community to think of personal issues and spiritual issues as one and the same.

When leading or speaking, be sure to include what issues you are working on as well, thus reinforcing the idea that personal growth is an ongoing process we are *all* in together. These communications could be about big or small things:

- I'm trying to spend less time at work so I can spend more time with my family.
- I'm trying to listen more and interrupt less.
- I'm focusing on letting my teenagers express their frustration without getting defensive.

- I'm trying to be more affectionate with my spouse.
- I'm trying to make a real meal a few times a week and sit down to eat as a family.
- I'm trying to say "I'm sorry" when I'm irritable at home.
- I'm trying to let people know when I'm upset instead of holding it against them.
- I'm not talking about my boss behind his back anymore.
- I'm bringing lunch once a week for a single mom in my office just to let her know someone's thinking about her.
- I'm learning to slow down and have more fun with my kids.
- When I get angry, I'm trying to walk away instead of exploding.
- I'm being more honest with God these days, telling him that I'm really frustrated with what's happening in my life.
- I'm asking God to help me understand that he accepts me.

Whether these goals sound spiritual or not, they are all about loving others better—being kinder, more patient, more self-controlled. It's about intentionally integrating biblical principles such as the fruit of the Spirit into your life. They must be practiced over and over until they become a habit, a part of who we are.

GETTING BEYOND BROKENNESS

You might want to regularly invite someone to share their journey during a service. This encourages others that change is possible and it reminds everyone about what we are at church to do. For instance, I interviewed John, who changed churches a few years ago and joined a men's process group recently. Here he talks about how his church's invitation to authentic community is changing his life:

> **What's been your experience with the church in regard to authenticity?**
>
> "In every church I've been a part of, there's been this expectation that when someone's been a Christian for ten years, fifteen years, they should be beyond certain things. So if you're

someone who is still dealing with things, you don't talk about it. You know how to do the right things, say the right things, because you only have to do them a certain amount of time each week when you're around other Christians. If you have issues, like me — and I've been a Christian for thirty years but I'm still wrestling with my anger — you tend to hide that because that's really a sign of weakness.

"So the first thing I heard coming to this church is that we are all broken and it's okay to be broken. Just the ability to say, 'Here's some of the stuff I'm dealing with,' is great. Being in this guys' group means I might find someone who is a half a step ahead of me. If I don't talk about my stuff, I'll never find the person who's dealing with the same things."

What was it like for you when you first started this men's group?

"Intimidating. Knowing that much about a guy puts a lot of pressure on me. That's a big commitment. I need to buy in first. To find out if I can trust the guys. If you try and pressure to get that buy-in too soon, it can push people away. Because guys are about fixing things. They don't want to come alongside too much. They want to fix it and move on. Give me your problem: I'll lay out an action plan and check back with you later. With this group, you have to be able to hear and say, 'I don't have an answer to that,' and be willing to walk through it with someone.

"One of the guys asked me, 'Why is it you never ask questions about me?' It was a brave question because we had met enough and we should have been to that level. I couldn't answer him till the next week. Then I told him, 'It's because I'm afraid that you're going to ask that same level of intimacy of me. That's my defense and I'm sorry about that. I am afraid but I'm okay with it.'"

So you find yourself resisting the process?

"At times I push myself to move. Most of the time, I find I let the guys pull me. The guys see me shut down. I still have questions about why I have to go back and discuss things from the past.

There's a large part of me that doesn't understand why I'm having to uncover this. I was raised with the idea that you don't let the past control you, you just put it behind you and move on. There's validity to that but I think I'm finding that the things that are in my past, that I have 'put behind me,' still affect the way I feel, the way I process things, interpret things, react to people. It really isn't put in the past. I don't know where that will lead me but it's got to be good."

What are you learning about yourself?

"As I'm writing stuff in the book [the *Leaving the Mud* workbook] or saying things in the group, I'm hearing myself express things I haven't heard myself express before. Holy crap, I didn't know that was in there. There was a question we had to answer, 'In your family of origin, what emotion was safe/easiest to express?' I found myself writing 'anger.' I thought that was weird, so I called my older brother and read him the question, and right away he said 'anger.' It was the most consistent emotion in our family. You knew it was always going to be there. What was hardest or most unsafe to express was compassion or love because you didn't know how that was going to be received. Usually it was received with sarcasm, which is why I do a lot of communication through sarcasm. Or it was outright ridiculed because it meant you were weak. Anger you got every day and you expected that. It was normal. So just answering that question, processing it, and talking to my brother helped me see that that has to be the reason anger is so easy for me to express. It's the safest thing. But I don't want that for my family, just expecting Dad to blow up."

Is it getting easier to express loving feelings?

"When my girls would bring home their report cards, with mostly A's, my way of expressing love was to say, 'What's with the B?' And my wife would look at me, and I would say, 'What? I'm just joking.' Because that's what we got at home. 'You could do better,' my mom would say. 'You're ugly, you're dumb' was her way of eliciting more from us."

Did you notice that your girls were hurt?

"I got that it wasn't what they wanted, but my logic was, that's what they need."

So the look on their face was irrelevant to you?

"Yeah, almost affirmation that I was doing the right thing."

So that puts you in this horrible spot. Your family is giving you feedback about how they are experiencing you, but you can't accept it.

"Yeah, you don't want feedback, you just want obedience. I had to learn that you want obedience to come from respect, not fear. I'm trying to break that cycle. Meeting with these guys helps me to process through these things. But telling your story, talking about your parents, feels disrespectful, like making excuses for your behavior. I don't want to do that."

It feels scary?

"Yeah. If I really start to explore my history, I don't know if I'm equipped to handle it. I don't know if the guys are equipped to handle it. It's like that movie, *Uncle Buck*. John Candy's got that old piece-of-junk car but it's working okay. I'm afraid that if I tear the engine apart, we won't be able to put it back together and I'll be left with just pain. We might end up saying, 'Man, that's a real mess. I'm not sure we should have done that.' It's safer just to shut it down. I'm not where I'd like to be with that.

"I'm seeing that I'm not as sensitive as I'd like to be. I like connecting with people but typically there's a point where the wall will come up, even with close friends. I usually do something to self-destruct—won't return phone calls, push people away. [I think,] 'You're learning a little too much about me. Maybe the real me might come out and I'm not sure we want that to happen.'

"I guess I don't know who the real me is. At an early age I had to become something and I had to earn approval from the people around me. I missed that part where my dad said, 'I'm really proud of you.' So I was always earning approval, always trying to become something for somebody else and that's probably still there. That's a lot of what we are trying to uncover through this process, so I don't know who the real me is. There's a lot of me that's afraid of that. I guess at some point I have to have faith in God to put the real me together the way he wants it to be and just trust him with that."

That's honest! John's authenticity about what it's like for him to be a part of a group gives people a realistic picture of the process—how scary it can be, how difficult it is to hang in and confront your fears, but also how life changing it is. It's easy to see that while it's hard, his investment is paying off. He's growing and the people in his life are benefiting from his effort.

YOUR TURN

1. What are your reactions to the perspectives/stories in this chapter?

(cont.)

2. What change do you most want to see in your community (for example: more accepting, more personal sharing, dealing with conflict, expressing doubts)?

3. Who in your community models authenticity? How might they help you create change in your environment?

If you're still with me, it's time to take a break from focusing on your community and return the focus to you. These final two chapters are about taking care of yourself while you do the intense work of creating an environment of authenticity. So, take a deep breath and relax. (Again, because I ask you to respond to some questions during the course of chapter 10, there is no "Your Turn" exercise at the end.)

Chapter 10
I'm Okay, No Really, I'm Okay
Letting yourself be human

By yourself you're unprotected. With a friend you can face the worst.

Ecclesiastes 4:12 (MSG)

The Lord makes firm the steps of those who delight in him; though they stumble, they will not fall, for the Lord upholds them with his hand.

Psalm 37:23 - 24

I'M NOT ALWAYS OKAY

It's quiet for a few minutes. Then I hear myself say, "My son stopped kissing me good-bye when he gets out of the car." I feel silly saying it and I worry that I might cry. But Belinda doesn't think I'm crazy. I can tell her anything. She just says, "Hmmm." Then, "Tell me when it happened." So I tell her, "The last two days when I dropped him off for school and then yesterday when I took him to soccer, he just got out of the car. I thought maybe he was just nervous about the first day of school, but what if he's done? What if he never kisses me good-bye again?" Belinda understands. She's already sent sons off to college. But more than that, she understands I need to tell my stories. So we talk about grief, and how being a mom is this huge defining thing until they leave us and then we have to figure out who we are all over again. She gets me and I feel so much better after being with her.

It's not a big thing, you know, just to say, "Tell me about it." And yet so many people can't or won't do it. Most are too busy or distracted or too uncomfortable to let the conversation go deeper. I desperately need people in my life who are not afraid, who will ask me how I am and actually want to hear the answer. Belinda does that. And she doesn't have to. She's my massage therapist. I found her "by accident" when my doctor recommended massage. Now I'm not sure what I would do without her. She's real and brave and wise, and I get so much more than what I pay for from her.

When you're a therapist or a church leader, you can go days or weeks without anybody noticing you're a person too, so you need people like Belinda in your life.

I was at a birthday party when my friend Debbie grabbed me and told me she'd been thinking about me for days. She said, "I felt all this compassion for you and all that you deal with. I just want you to know, I see you." It stunned me. Out of the blue like that, with no agenda, while I was trying so hard to be light and funny, she saw me. And it was such a relief. Like I could finally take a breath after being underwater too long.

I feel bad about needing so much from others, wanting to be seen, listened to sometimes. I'm not supposed to. I come from good Mennonite stock. I know how to work hard. I know how to go without. In fact, I am happiest when I work till I fall over. This is not healthy, as my husband has told me many times. But when I'm exhausted it means I've done all I can. I can't physically carry on any longer, so it's okay to finally rest. Church culture fosters this same attitude. If we're really serving God, it ought to cost us something; it ought to include some suffering.

And it will. Whether we serve as an overfunctioner—out of touch with ourselves but busy—or we serve from an authentic, healthy place, working with people will be intense. Of course, the more authentic and healthy we are, the more effective our work will be. But being involved deeply with others can often be overwhelming. So how do we do it for the long haul?

LEARNING TO DO SELF-CARE

Therapists talk about "self-care" which, to us, means being aware of and taking responsibility for our own condition. We take this task seriously because we know if we don't, we will end up hurting the people we are trying to serve. It means exploring and addressing our own emotional and spiritual issues so they don't get in the way. And pacing ourselves physically so that we've got enough energy to be fully present for each client. It's about learning to manage the things that use up our energy and at the same time making room for things that feed our soul, or give us energy.

You are not just a means to everybody else's transformation. This adventure you're on, this mission to change the world just a little bit, is also about your own transformation. And while other work might be getting done along the way, your own personal work won't if you are constantly moving at the speed of light. Your growth requires that you, like those you serve, pause long enough to feel your own life, evaluate your own relationships, explore your thoughts and attitudes, and create strategies for change.

Here are some questions to get you thinking about your own self-care:

1. What do you do that feeds your soul?

2. What do you do for fun? When was the last time you did it?

3. How often do you spend time with close friends? What is that like for you?

4. Who makes up your support system? Who nurtures you? What is it about them that provides nurture?

_____
_____
_____
_____

5. How often do you laugh hard? With whom?

_____
_____
_____
_____

6. How often do you get a good night's sleep?

_____
_____
_____
_____

7. How do you feel physically? How's your body doing? Do you suffer from headaches? Muscle tension? Stomach problems? Had any vegetables lately?

_____
_____
_____
_____

8. What do you do to get some exercise? How often?

_____
_____
_____
_____

9. What do you do to quiet yourself? How often does that happen?

_____
_____
_____
_____

I know some of these questions are irritating, the kind your mother might ask. But she'd ask them because they're important. If you don't take care of yourself, everyone else will suffer eventually. We have seen it over and over: leaders who burn out or end up sabotaging themselves because they weren't paying any attention to their own needs and issues. That's a big mess to clean up. So please, take care of yourself. We need you!

CREATING BOUNDARIES, SAYING NO

A starting place for self-care might be putting some boundaries in place. Look critically at your schedule. What could go? Maybe a program or meeting that isn't very effective? Maybe a relationship that doesn't seem to be going anywhere? What can you cancel? What could you do less of, at least for a while? What could you delegate to others? Maybe there are some big time-wasters that you need to limit—Internet browsing, video games, TV. Maybe an hour or so helps you relax but two or three hours of it paralyzes you.

Initially saying no to things and people is terrifying; it can feel totally wrong and selfish. And not everyone will be happy about it because it's not what they're used to. That's okay. You are trying to live authentically and make choices that are healthy. Choices that will help you be more loving. More real in a few relationships rather than spread thin, accomplishing little, in many superficial ones. Saying no to some things allows you to say yes to others and actually allows you to care for people more effectively. But in the moment it feels like the most loving response to someone's request is to say yes. However, saying yes at the wrong time to the wrong thing results in us feeling overwhelmed and resentful. Making more thoughtful decisions frees us to give wholeheartedly rather than out of obligation.

Consider the following boundary-setting questions to help you get specific:

1. How many appointments or meetings can you do a week and still be emotionally present and effective?
2. How often and how much time alone per week do you need to feel centered?

3. How often do you need to see close friends to feel seen and heard?
4. How much time can you devote to a crisis without getting exhausted? How do you know when it's time to pull back a little?

Everyone's answers to these questions will be different. It doesn't matter what those answers are, just that you know them and respect them. Even if you don't like what you discover about yourself. My friend Kathy Escobar (from the Refuge) can do more in an hour than I can do in a day. She copastors a church and raises five children and she's happy about it! I wish I could do that, but I can't. Some of the therapists in my office can see ten clients in a day. I can't do that either. When I try, things get ugly: I feel shaky all the time, don't sleep well, and nobody really gets what they need from me. So I'm learning to embrace a pace that works for me.

I know I can only see about fifteen clients a week, that I need to see my girlfriends regularly, and that I need to spend hours every day hanging out with my family. I need downtime, exercise time, alone time. If I keep things manageable most of the time, I have enough energy for the occasional crisis — which is always just around the corner. I can tolerate stretches which require greater intensity because I'm not totally used up by my everyday life.

Whatever you need, it's okay. Life is not a competition. You are not failing if you can't keep up with someone else. We're aiming for quality, not quantity. Our goal is to function so that our communities, families, and friends get the best we have to offer.

If you haven't read the book *Boundaries* by Henry Cloud and John Townsend, I recommend it. One of their most helpful concepts for me is the idea of "boulders versus knapsacks" based on Galatians 6:2, 5. Cloud and Townsend describe boulders as burdens people have to bear that are too difficult to carry alone, such as the death of a loved one, an accident, a sudden financial crisis, an affair. These events can be crushing if others don't come alongside and help. When they happen, it's appropriate for us to drop everything and do what we can to provide comfort and support to the person carrying the boulder. Knapsacks are different. Cloud and Townsend describe them as "the everyday things we all need to do." We all have responsibilities that are our own to fulfill, such as getting ourselves to work, taking care of our homes and children, paying the bills. Getting clear on the difference between the two kinds of loads is important because carrying someone else's knapsack is counterproductive. It teaches people that they don't have to take care of their own responsibilities, and it exhausts and causes resentment for those who are doing the work for them.[8]

While we sometimes confuse knapsacks for boulders, it's pretty hard to miss an honest-to-goodness boulder when it hits. Like the one that dropped on some friends of ours recently.

A CRUSHING BOULDER

Our daughter Katie's friend Ben just turned eighteen. Today he's in the hospital with a brain tumor, something none of us knew he had a week ago. He and his mom had tried to get help for his headaches before but the doctor never bothered to check his brain. Yesterday Ben and his family were told that the tumor will eventually kill him. We are all in shock. Katie is a mess. She can't eat, cries through all her classes, then races to the hospital at noon and stays there till they kick her out.

I've spent the better part of the last four days at the hospital, as have many others. As horrible as it is, there is so much beauty going on in that hospital room. Twenty or so high schoolers are there at any given time. They stay for hours, huddled into each other, alternately crying and laughing, quietly talking. When the doctors come in, they shuffle off to the lobby, wait for as long as it takes, then shuffle back into his room. The first night Ben's water polo team showed up. These beautiful, strong young men cried and held him one at a time. They prayed for him in these broken little-boy voices, begging God to rescue their friend. These moments are so big, so sacred, they are hard to bear.

These kids are so alive. They are not afraid to love deeply or to need each other desperately. And to say so. Ben tells them over and over he wants them all there, that he needs them, and collectively they say, "Of course we will be with you. There's nowhere else we could be right now." They bring Ben stuffed animals, Snickers bars, Jamba Juice, and last night, for some reason, a beta fish. They skip school and sneak in to play Guitar Hero at 8:00 a.m. Clearly, twenty-five kids in one hospital room is over the limit, but the nurses can't bring themselves to enforce the rules. They have been won over by the power of love. All of us have. We adults find ourselves guarding the door when visiting hours are over, helping the kids craft *Mission Impossible*–style plans to sneak into Ben's room in the middle of the night to make sure he doesn't feel alone. We can't bear to see them separated. It's a beautiful thing, the way they love each other.

The grown-ups are doing what we can—finding specialists, calling people we know who've had brain tumors, searching the Internet for treatment options and cutting-edge facilities. We are loving on Debbie and Paul and his sister Sierra the best we can. This is a huge boulder. Too big for Ben, too big for his family, and so we drop everything to bear it together.

Of course, sometimes the line between boulder and knapsack is blurry and we are not sure when getting involved will end up biting us in the butt instead of making a difference for someone. It's okay to take some time to decide. If you can, look at the patterns in this person's life. Is crisis something that keeps happening to them? Do they bring it on by their own choices? Are they always struggling just to take care of their regular responsibilities, always looking for someone to take over for them? Is this something they cannot or will not do for themselves?

My friend Beth told me about an agency she used to work for that required helpers to use only resources that were available to their clients. For example, if they wanted to accompany a client to a doctor's appointment or sign up for welfare, the helper must use the same transportation available to the client. Using the helper's car would have meant making the client more dependent rather than building the client's ability to solve their own problems (carry their own knapsack) with a little support. The idea is that instead of taking people's problems from them, we stand beside them and look at the problem together, asking exploring-type questions such as: what have you tried, how did that work out, what else might you try, how do you think that will go? This likely will take some practice getting used to.

Karen, a therapist in my office who often teaches on boundaries, suggests not giving an answer when someone asks for something you are not sure you can give. She encourages getting in the habit of saying, "Let me get back to you about that," so that you have some time to really think about what's best for the other person *and* what's doable for you. This has been a life saver for me. It's okay to ask people to wait while you consider how to respond. Your life is serious business and ought to be lived as intentionally as possible. Remember that whatever you decide, you still need time and energy to take care of your own life and family. If helping others means consistently abandoning your own responsibilities, you are too involved.

Sometimes helpers lean in the opposite direction. They get so burnt out over time that they stop getting involved much at all, even ignoring the boulders they see around them. When this happens, you have too many boundaries. If you are lacking friendships and other mutually satisfying relationships, it may be because your boundaries have become too rigid to let anyone in.

MAKING PEACE WITH STRESS

No matter how good we get at using our boundaries and trying to pace ourselves, working with people will often keep us just inches away from being overwhelmed. Bad stuff happens and people need our support, and sometimes that will mean going without sleep or time alone or fun in order to help carry a burden for others. That's the way it goes. What's been helpful for me is accepting that I've chosen a path that sometimes gets intense. But that intensity is connected to what makes my life meaningful.

I learned this in the middle of the night a few years ago. That night, I was lying wide awake at 3:00 a.m., too stressed to sleep. The reason for my stress was that in a few days I was supposed to present a workshop on managing stress to a group of women and I still had nothing to say. (It's kind of funny, if it's not happening to *you*.)

It wasn't just a lack of a presentation that was bothering me. The six months leading up to this event had been a little crazy. For starters, in October, Kathy (from the Refuge) and I had signed a contract with a retreat center to do our own women's retreat. It was something we had been dreaming about for a while and the place we wanted had an opening. Unfortunately, the weekend available was only three months away. In that amount of time, the two of us would have to write all the material, create a workbook, do marketing, registration, find facilitators, organize small groups, and so on. Signing the contract meant promising the camp thousands of dollars regardless of how many women showed up. We were nervous but felt we were supposed to move forward, so we did.

A few weeks later, in the middle of Thanksgiving week and the mad scramble to pull this all together, one of my closest friends was diagnosed with cancer! Deanna was only thirty-seven at the time and the "C" word came out of the blue. She'd been feeling tired, achy, and nauseous for about a year. Finally, after many attempts to find out what was wrong, the doctors found a mass in one of her kidneys and she was immediately scheduled for surgery.

It's always a horrible shock to hear that someone you love has a life-threatening condition. It's like a bad dream you can't wake up from. You can't breathe or think; you can only feel. One of the things I was feeling was mad. I mean, really mad. How could God do this? To Deanna and her children! To us! Most specifically, to me! I remember sitting in her living room a few days later. She was so calm, it was unnerving. She described this sense of peace she had, despite her expectation that there would be more bad news after surgery. She talked about dying and how she was ready to accept that.

I know I should have been relieved, grateful that God was so present for her, carrying her through this, but it totally freaked me out! I wanted to scream, "How can you do this to me? You can't die! Stop talking about dying!" Instead I grabbed her and sobbed. Some for her, but honestly, mostly for me.

And I argued with God: "You can't be serious. After all we've been through, you're going to take her away from me? I need her! She gets me. Do you know how hard it is to find someone who gets me?" The thought of growing old without her put me in a panic. But Deanna was preparing to die, whether I was ready or not. In the days before the operation she ran around town, returning anything she could so there'd be more money for Dan and the kids after her death. She even refused to buy a new pair of pajamas for the hospital because she didn't want to waste the money! That day, I'm embarrassed to say, I lost it. I screamed at her, "Buy the damn pajamas! If you die, *I* will give Dan the forty bucks!" Then I cried again.

And then came the operation ... and amazingly good news—they got it all, no need for treatments! As quickly as cancer had overtaken our lives, it vanished!

A few weeks later, we were at the retreat! Hundreds of details taken care of, materials written and printed, ladies all assembled. I remember how surreal it felt, standing there in front of them that Friday night, with Deanna there in the front row grinning from ear to ear. By the time the weekend was over, it was clear that as hard as it had been to make it to that point, God had had plans for the retreat and somehow what we'd just been through was a part of it.

Then I returned home—to a house remodel! Me, Ken, Katie, and Josh and all our earthly possessions squished into just a few bedrooms of our house. No kitchen, no heat, no space to move, no place to sit. I was trying to be a good sport about it, since it was my idea. And I was, until the few days prior to my workshop on stress—that night I couldn't sleep.

I was mad that night too. And I was complaining to God about how this was all just way too much: "The last six months have been exhausting. In three days I'm supposed to do this thing and I've got nothing to say. How do you expect me to handle all of this? I need you to give me something for these ladies! I can't show up with nothing to say!"

And then the strangest thing happened! God began to tell me something. (Now I was raised in the Baptist tradition and I know God is not supposed to talk specifically to me but sometimes he does anyway. Clearly, God is not Baptist.)

In my head flashes this picture of a roller coaster and all the people on it have their hands in the air, screaming and smiling. And I hear these words, "It's a wild ride, isn't it?" And I say, "Clever, God, but not very funny." But he's not done. He brings to mind Deanna and the cancer scare, and he says something like this, "You finally have a friend in your life who you love enough to be terrified of losing. Isn't that great?" And I remembered the way life used to be before Deanna and Debbie and Kathy, when there were no women in my life who meant that much to me. Then he brought to mind my work and said, "You have work that allows you to be authentic and create growth in people's lives, and sometimes the weight of that responsibility keeps you up at night. Isn't that great?" And I remembered how bored I used to be, how I had longed for work that would fully engage me and make a difference in the lives of others. He brought to mind other things too and, in the end, I saw his point clearly. Years ago I had begged God for the life that I was sitting smack dab in the middle of. And while it was intense, it was also everything I had longed for.

I have always been afraid of too much intensity. I don't want to feel too much because then I'm not in control. I like things to be safe and predictable. I like to feel the ground under my feet. I don't understand people who like roller coasters and I particularly don't understand the ones who throw their arms up during a free fall! That's crazy! I want to scream "What are you thinking? Hold on to the bar! Don't you read the papers?" But that night God was teaching me a lesson I desperately needed to learn. That what he has created me for and given to me is a life of meaning and intensity, where things, though not always manageable or easy, are real and significant. I could go back to living disconnected from others, so that when they got cancer I would only be sad instead of terrified. I could have a job that didn't require authenticity from me or involve walking through pain with people. I could say no to doing everything that scared me. But I had that life before, and I was really BORED!

So I have been changing the way I look at stress and trying to make peace with the intensity in my life. And I want to invite you to rethink your own. To differentiate between stress that's a result of doing too much of the wrong stuff and the intensity that comes from giving your life to things you believe in, that you were born for. The problem is not just that we are too busy (though, absolutely, we often are), but that we are too busy doing too many things we don't believe in.

So keep evaluating. Are you giving your life, your time, your energy to things you believe in, or are you giving yourself to things *other* people believe in? As often as you can, say no to anything you don't believe in. Yes, people will be disappointed, but aren't some people already disappointed in us no matter how hard we try? The sooner we accept that we will never be able to fulfill everyone's expectations, the sooner we will be free to live intentionally.

But do say yes, no matter what, to anything God calls you to. If you sense God is nudging you toward something, go—even if you are scared! That's where the good stuff is, where your passions will be fanned back to life and your creativity will be expressed. You don't want to miss it. Just be as sure as possible that God has called you to it. Take some time to get clear about it. Then jump in with both feet and prepare yourself for intensity to follow.

A couple more things: Take care of your body. You need it to carry you around. I'm not talking about working out so you look like a movie star. Just acknowledge that your body needs some regular TLC and give yourself permission to do what it takes to stay strong.

Hold somebody once in a while—your kids, your spouse, strangers on the street. Touch is powerfully healing and calming. Sometimes when I feel the pressure building, I grab one of my kids and just hold on to them for a little bit. Just having them close, feeling their love, giving them mine, centers me. It reminds me that whatever else is going on, we have each other. It energizes me and gives me courage to keep rolling.

And lastly, once in a while, laugh hard enough to pee your pants. (I find this gets easier as you get older.) When was the last time you laughed that hard? If it was high school, that's way too long ago. Laughing helps change your perspective. Crack a joke in the middle of a stressful moment and watch it change everyone's mood. It clears the air and gives people new energy to tackle what's in front of them.

Whenever you can, spend an evening with friends who like to laugh and just let yourself go—laugh till you cry, till you have a bellyache ... or till you pee your pants.

The longer you practice setting boundaries, the easier it will be. Eventually people will realize that you are taking your life seriously. That your family, health, and soul are important and need attending to. They will learn to accept, maybe even admire, your boundaries and to respect your commitment. You will begin to have more energy, less anxiety and resentment. You'll sleep better, feel more creative, and enjoy your life more.

Look for God in the middle of your wild ride. He is there, cheering you on and holding down the bar so you won't fall out.

CHAPTER 11

When Denial Is a Good Thing
Refusing to give up

"I will go before you and will level the mountains; I will break down gates of bronze and cut through bars of iron. I will give you the treasures of darkness, riches stored in secret places, so that you may know that I am the LORD, the God of Israel, who summons you by name."

Isaiah 45:2-3

I'm supposed to be writing all day today, but instead I'm reading a novel about menopausal women. College roommates reunited after thirty years. It's not particularly good, but it's better than trying to write. People often think that writing just magically happens. Maybe it does for some people, but not for me.

Here's how it will go down.

First I will look at the monitor for a long time, with no ideas whatsoever. Then I will reread what I was last working on only to discover that it's total crap and will have to be rewritten. Then I will wander to the kitchen, pretending I am hungry. I'll say to myself, "Once I have a little something, I will be energized. Maybe I'll have some nuts. Nuts are good for you. I'll have the chocolate covered ones; after all, chocolate is a vegetable."

Then I'll go back to the computer, stare at the screen again for a long time, and write a few paragraphs that I know I will hate tomorrow. Right about then I will be sliding into the miserable-yet-familiar pit of despair. I will spend several hours agonizing over what a huge disappointment I will be to anyone who reads this. I will panic a little: "What will happen when people discover I am a complete fraud?" Next comes, "If only I could say something profound like Anne Lamott or Donald Miller, then this agony might be worth it." Then the awareness hits that I have wasted hours, accomplished nothing, AND my butt is getting bigger. I will start thinking about making a doctor's appointment to ask for an antidepressant. This will go on and on until someone in my family comes home to rescue me.

You can see why I might avoid writing. As it is, I'd rather take a sharp stick to the eye and be done with it. I sometimes wish I were a narcissist. I know they're hard to live with, but wouldn't it be great to go through life thinking you're amazing? I mean, can you imagine waking up every morning and marveling at how brilliant you are? Think how much more you could get done in a day without wasting all that time trying to talk yourself into offering what you've got to the world?

Instead, it's often a struggle. Most of us have some version of this sort of self-rejecting, self-loathing thing going on from time to time. Doubting yourself seems to come with the territory. Working with people involves a lot of guesswork. It's complicated, hard to measure, and never finished. Certainly there are glorious moments, like when a couple recommits to one another, or someone with an addiction takes an important step toward recovery, or a small group shows up to care for someone in crisis. But there's never a time when everyone's happy all at once and we can sit back to breathe a sigh of relief over a job well done. The work is rife with opportunities to feel incompetent and inadequate because we are trying to do something big. Bigger than us, bigger than programs and services. We are trying to create real, lasting life change.

But life change can and does happen, and when it does, it's magnificent! Being a part of it is hugely fulfilling. And you don't have to be a superstar to make a difference. You just have to want it enough to keep moving toward it. For yourself and for others.

What separates the men from the boys in terms of emotional health and spiritual maturity is courage and perseverance. I've watched it over and over as I work with people. It's not about how smart they are, what books they've read, or what seminars they've attended. Bottom line—the people who grow and change do so because they just refuse to give up. They keep fighting against the urge to accept their brokenness as their identity. Sure, they have days when they want to throw in the towel, but they always get back in the game and give it another shot. They do the only thing there is to do if you're going to take your one-and-only life seriously—they try again. We can be among those people who experience progress by being willing to engage in the struggle long term. We will have to decide over and over to get up again after falling down, to just keep pressing on, regardless of our rate of success, regardless of the odds against us—even if all we can do is take one baby step at a time.

A LESSON FROM JOSHUA AND THE ISRAELITES

Think of the Old Testament Israelites wandering in the desert. After generations of slavery in Egypt at last they have been delivered. But they can't pull it together to join God in his rescue effort. The Promised Land is there in front of them yet they are too afraid to take it. They have been slaves for so long they can't imagine themselves as anything else. They can't let go of that mentality long enough to claim a land of their own, a home, a place where they could finally be free.

But then along comes Joshua, a new kind of leader. The book of Joshua opens with his story. By now, the Israelites have totally lost their vision and are just plain lost! And have been for forty years. In fact, the generation of adults who experienced the dramatic exodus through the Red Sea are dying off. Moses is gone and leadership has been passed on to Joshua, who was still young when the Israelites left Egypt. Amazingly, though he's grown up during the wilderness years, he still believes in God's promise of abundance for the chosen nation. He refuses to accept the desert as their home. He refuses to give up. And so God calls him to lead, tells him it's time to move, to finally claim what has been waiting for them:

> Now then, you and all these people, get ready to cross the Jordan River into the land I am about to give to them.... I will give you

every place where you set your foot, as I promised Moses.... No one will be able to stand against you all the days of your life. As I was with Moses, so I will be with you; I will never leave you nor forsake you. Be strong and courageous, because you will lead these people to inherit the land I swore to their ancestors to give them. Be strong and very courageous (Joshua 1: 2–7).

This new generation is inspired by Joshua's courage and determination. They take a first step. They move out, into the Jordan River, and God rewards their courage by parting the waters and leading them safely across. The river behind them, they are confronted with the task of taking the land from its inhabitants—first, the city of Jericho, with its huge walls. It's a crazy mission. God delivers these wacky instructions: a combination of walking, walking, walking, blowing trumpets, and yelling. Can you imagine? It must have been nearly impossible to believe that this was really God's idea and yet they proceed, against all odds—against the walls and the city and its army, against their own fear of failure, against a history of cowardice and aimless wandering. And the city falls! Victory after victory is recorded in the book of Joshua as the Israelities continue to respond to God's direction to occupy the Promised Land.

Why this generation? Why not those who had witnessed the plagues, the parting of the Red Sea? I've heard people argue that those Israelites were lazy, faithless, and apathetic, content to live in the desert. I don't think so. I think they knew this wasn't all there was but the task ahead was just so big. I think they were a lot like me—afraid. It's true they had witnessed God's power in supernatural ways, but I have too. While I haven't been led by a flaming pillar or received manna dropped out of the sky, I have seen him at work in my life and the lives of others in amazing ways. And yet the minute he puts a new challenge in front of me, I want to run. My first response, my prevailing response, is fear. What if God doesn't show up this time? If I take a step, if I jump off this cliff, how do I know he'll catch me? It's a fair question because, truly, things that God has called me to in the past have not always gone well. Sometimes they have been confusing, frustrating, and loaded with difficulties. And yet regardless of the results, it still seemed the path he wanted me to take.

TAKING THE RISK

Some of the work of therapy involves encouraging people to take a risk. It's safer to stay stuck than to let go of patterns or strategies we are used to and comfortable with. We may hate them and understand that they keep us from growing, but it's easier to live in familiar misery than to hope again that we might be able to change. Often we are like the wilderness generation who had no dreams, no power, and kept saying, "We can't do it." Dan Allender, author of *The Wounded Heart*, says that when we have been wounded we learn to stop hoping for our future; we stop dreaming about what could be in our lives. Hoping and dreaming feel like a setup for failure and we don't want to be disappointed again, so we give it up.[9] But hoping and dreaming is exactly what we need to do.

Children know how to dream and we can learn a lot about living just by watching them. Years ago, when our kids, Katie and Josh, were eleven and nine, they decided, along with their friends, Amanda and Kevan, to start a band. They had a name for their group; they wrote songs; they planned rehearsal sessions, for which I was to make cupcakes. They were quite sure that soon they would begin traveling the country and become very famous. They got together often to talk about how great it was to be a band. Without actually ever singing or making music of any kind, they maintained their excitement about being a band for several months. It was irrelevant to them that none of them could play an instrument or knew anything about music. What made them a band was simply their dream to be one. The impossible meant nothing to them!

The impossible means nothing to God either. Whatever we believe about ourselves, at least this much is true: you and I are no longer slaves. While we may lose our way sometimes, we are not lost. God knows where we are and he has a journey in mind for each of us. He will never stop wooing us toward restoration and freedom, and he promises enough strength for whatever work he calls us to.

God is waiting to do something more in our generation, in our families, in our church communities. I don't want to be like the wilderness generation, too afraid to deal with my stuff to join God in his plan for me. I don't want to leave a legacy of fear and stagnation. I want to pass on courage and perseverance so that my children will know how to be brave, how to face the parts of themselves that need healing and restoration, how to move out when God calls them.

Some of us have a Jordan River to cross or a Jericho to conquer in our own lives and we are scared. We want to know before moving on how this whole thing will turn out—whether we'll be successful, what it will look like on the other side. But God doesn't usually give us that. Instead he gives us manna—just what we need for today. And as scary as that is, it can be enough.

YOUR TURN

1. What might be your Jordan River, your Jericho — something God is calling you to confront in your life? What help might you need to put into place to begin dealing with your challenge?

2. What are you afraid might happen if you accept your challenge?

3. What is your sense of what God might be asking of you, in terms of how you lead?

4. What are your fears of trying to make any changes at your church? What might happen? Who might be resistant or unsupportive?

5. What kind of support would you need to take these steps of change? Who might you rely on for support?

I value your thoughts about what you've just read.
Please share them with me. You'll find contact information
in the back of this book.

Notes

1. Brennan Manning, *Abba's Child*, rev. ed. (Colorado Springs: NavPress, 2002), 21–22.
2. Shawn Coyle, *To Hell with Church* (n.p.: Slathering Dog Books, 2005), 4.
3. Peter Scazzero, *The Emotionally Healthy Church* (Grand Rapids, Mich.: Zondervan, 2003), 18–19.
4. Harriet Lerner, *The Dance of Anger* (New York: Harper & Row, 1985), 192.
5. Ibid.
6. Ibid., 193.
7. Patrick Carnes, *Contrary to Love* (Minneapolis: CompCare Publishers, 1989), summary from ch. 5.
8. Henry Cloud and John Townsend, *Boundaries*, paperback ed. (Grand Rapids, Mich.: Zondervan, 2002), 30–31.
9. Dan B. Allender, *The Wounded Heart* (Colorado Springs: NavPress, 1995), 103.

Share Your Thoughts

With the Author: Your comments will be forwarded to the author when you send them to *zauthor@zondervan.com*.

With Zondervan: Submit your review of this book by writing to *zreview@zondervan.com*.

Free Online Resources at www.zondervan.com/hello

Zondervan AuthorTracker: Be notified whenever your favorite authors publish new books, go on tour, or post an update about what's happening in their lives.

Daily Bible Verses and Devotions: Enrich your life with daily Bible verses or devotions that help you start every morning focused on God.

Free Email Publications: Sign up for newsletters on fiction, Christian living, church ministry, parenting, and more.

Zondervan Bible Search: Find and compare Bible passages in a variety of translations at www.zondervanbiblesearch.com.

Other Benefits: Register yourself to receive online benefits like coupons and special offers, or to participate in research.